About him, for her . . .

EROTIC ASTROLOGY

OLIVIA

D0035319

Ballantine Books • New York

All rights reserved under International and Pan-American Copyright Conventions. Published in the United States by Ballantine Books, a division of Random House, Inc., New York, and distributed in Canada by Random House of Canada Limited, Toronto. Originally published by Victoria House Press in 1995.

http://www.randomhouse.com

Library of Congress Catalog Card Number: 96-97080

ISBN: 0-345-40978-7

Cover design by Kristine V. Mills-Noble
Cover photos: Top. © Mark Adams/Westlight. Bottom. © Barnaby Hall/Photonica

Manufactured in the United States of America

First Ballantine Books Edition: February 1997

10 9 8 7 6 5 4 3 2 1

To Jeanne Moreau who said:
"Sex is a search; sensuality is a quest."

CONTENTS

SOME STARRY NIGHT...

You will find the man who makes your body feel as finely tuned as a Stradivarius. The one lover in the world who can touch your soul.

What will you do to mesmerize him, to make him your own?

This book can help you do just that...by lifting the veil on the mysterious world of erotic astrology.

Now you will know what sexual pleasures your lover fantasizes. What turns him on and off. Is there a special food that loosens his libido? A color that sparks his erotic fantasies? What part of his body will be most sensitive to your touch?

Most important, Olivia will tell you what unique pleasures will delight him in bed. Sensations that will make having sex with you as important as the air he breathes.

The art of erotic sex...

Make no mistake about it, it is an art...based on the full exploration of your five senses. You will learn how to heighten your own and your lover's sense of hearing, sight, smell, taste and touch.

Finally, you will understand that when it comes to the senses in love making, it is the mind that makes the most sense of all. By using the powers of your mind and letting your imagination soar, you can guide your lover to sexual heights neither of you knew existed.

Erotic sex means doing everything just a little bit slower.

The first lesson is that you never, never force-feed the erotic.

It must be like French pastry: light, delicious and seductive.
The way you walk into a room, pour the wine, blow out a candle, stroke his arm...all just a little bit slower and far more sensuous.

Of course, when it comes to making love too quickly, the
male of the species is usually more guilty than we females. With
rare exception, we are all perfectly happy to spend time in slow,
sensual foreplay. We want to explore fingertips for countless
minutes. We love to be stroked...sensually...excruciatingly...for
hours.

Most men, on the other hand, whose bodies naturally acceler-
ate quicker, have a harder job learning the slow, tantalizing
dance of erotic sex. They're like over excited children on a first
long trip, asking every ten minutes: "Are we there yet??"

Olivia will help you teach him to slow down when the foreplay goes over 10 miles an hour...to enjoy a view or two...
knowing the destination will be all the more delicious because
he took the time to stop...to smell...to touch...to taste the roses!

But how does astrology help you teach the art of erotic sex?

The infinite variety of the zodiac...

If the man in your life is a Scorpio, you will learn never to let
your sexual relationship get stuck in the old, ho-hum missionary position. Sharing an erotic art book with a Capricorn is a
strong sexual turn on, but, trust Olivia, it is much better suited
to a Libra lover. However, reading steamy erotic passages from
Henry Miller with a Virgo is incredible foreplay.

Do all men born under the same astrological sign have the
same sexual desires?

Every man under the sun is uniquely different. There are
twelve houses in an astrological chart. Each house signifies a
different part of life: marriage, health, career, home and so on.
Different planets are found in each of the houses, plus each
house falls under the influence of a different astrological sign of
the zodiac. So you see, your lover is a fascinating blend of complex cosmic influences.

I purposely didn't advise which female sign is most compatible with a male sign. That's because even if your lover has a
Capricorn sun, he may have many planets in Pisces. In that case
he's going to exhibit strong Piscean characteristics.

Now, what happens when an Aries female, madly in love with this Capricorn, picks up an astrology magazine and reads that Aries doesn't mesh with Capricorn? Should she panic? Is what seemed like the ideal union over before it's begun?

Happily, the heavens are not that simple.

It's true that at first glance Aries and Capricorn may not be the most compatible of signs, but what if her own astrological chart shows many planets in Capricorn? Or even in Pisces? See what I mean? She would have many things in common with this lover, and their union would probably turn out to be as erotically blessed as she had hoped.

So remember, even though astrology magazines may tell you certain sun signs are not compatible -- astrology is infinitely complex -- and personalized charts can change the whole picture.

The ascendant can only be known when the birth time is known.

What makes this so important? The ascendant is the "face" that we show to the world, our outer personality. It is the sign rising on the eastern horizon at the exact moment of birth.

After reading the different signs in this book, you might think that your lover's personality seems a lot more like, let's say, an impulsive Aries than the cautious Capricorn you know him to be. Once you know his personalized chart, you just may discover that his ascendant is Aries.

If you know the date of your lover's birth, the place he was born, and can find out the exact time (it's usually on his birth certificate) you can obtain his personal horoscope showing the placement of all his planets, plus his rising sign or ascendant. (See the last page in the back of this book.)

A personal chart will give you an in-depth look at what's really under his skin. If you can't find out the specific time he was born, his sun sign, on which I have based the profiles in this book, will still divulge fascinating material.

A gift of erotic love...

Yes, it's been said so many times -- but it can never be said enough. Before you seduce this man's mind, body, heart and soul, make sure that he's been tested and is Aids free. I suggest that you give him that same gift in return.

Then, because the disease can lie dormant for so long, still use a condom. They come in a fascinating variety of colors and flavors. Experiment and see which ones do the most for your erotic taste buds.

Share the fantasy...

Erotic Astrology will also introduce you to your lover's sexual fantasy world. Don't be shy about entering this fascinating playground. After all, your man has many wild facets to his personality (that's what you love about him, isn't it?) and by playing different roles and letting your imagination run equally wild -- you'll be helping him to express them all. Not to mention the fact that you'll be satisfying your own sexual pleasures immeasurably.

So act out fantasies with the joy of an actress who knows her art...and knows that she's playing to the most appreciative audience in the world! Naturally, after you enter *his* fantasy world, your lover will want to peek inside yours. Imagine discovering that you both dream of different roles in the same fantasy! And they say that Christmas only comes once a year!

And so, one starry night...

Somewhere in the future, you will be lying in your lover's arms. He will breathe into your ear that sex has been so incredible, so magical, that your relationship must have been made in heaven.

He'll never know how right he is.

ARIES

MAR 21 – APR 19

RULING PLANET: MARS

MASCULINE, POSITIVE FIRE SIGN

EROTIC DRIVE: TO CONQUER

COLOR: RED

PASSION FLOWER: HYACINTH

MAGIC SCENT: GINGER

GEM: DIAMOND

METAL: IRON

HERBS:

Broom   Holy Thistle   Honeysuckle

> *"It is not enough to conquer,*
> *one must know how to seduce."*
> **Voltaire**

Ah Aries, without you there would be no thrill of adventure, no mountains to climb, no savage corporate worlds to conquer.

This fire sign, ruled by Mars, is impulsive and passionate. He is a doer who plunges into whatever excites him and lives to either regret it or celebrate it. He is legendary for shooting first and counting casualties later. However, I must tell you that he is also famous for a divine kind of courage. The kind that lets him dare adventures lesser mortals only dream about.

Your Aries lover (whose symbol is the "horny" Ram) is masculine from his hair, often reddish due to the ruler Mars, down to his size twelves. And even if he isn't blessed with a compelling physique, rest assured that he is every inch a warrior.

It's even probable that your lover has a beard, or is deciding whether to grow one or to cut one off. If he has a choice, he'll wear his hair on the long side (Sampson, with his ego and strength in his mane was probably an Aries!) A born athlete, he is also extremely aware of his body image. Many an Aries male can be found at the gym, pretending to be unaware of the females who are pretending to be unaware of his glistening pecs.

As your relationship begins to develop, you'll find that Aries is more comfortable in the dominant role. Yes, Olivia means in *that* dominant position too, but right now we're talking about normal he-she role playing. However, beneath his macho facade there is a strong need for your approval. Am I really good enough to reach the top of that mountain? Do I have the courage? Do I have the skill?

Aries looks into your eyes for the answer.

WHAT TURNS HIM ON?

For starters, this man loves the thrill of the chase and the moment of conquest more than the bounty itself. So I suggest you put on running shoes and make this lover work up a decent sweat before succumbing.

Then, to seduce him heart, mind, body and soul, try a little well-aimed flattery. Stroke his ego by telling him how complete he makes you feel; how incredibly lucky you are that he came into your life. Since Aries has all the humility of Donald Trump, he will be thrilled that a female exists with so much good taste!

The big turn on for Aries is discovering someone who is not predictable. Your man loves a unique personality (which he equates with his own, of course) who is stimulating, where-the-action-is, and energetic enough to keep up with him. You probably know by now that Aries loves fast cars, but be aware that his own mental motor is usually running at 200 mph. That's enough of a challenge for any hot-blooded female. His motor, by the way, isn't always propelled by physical energy. The philosopher, Joseph Campbell, was a famed Aries.

WHAT TURNS HIM OFF?

As I told you, females who are predictable have a short life span with this lover. Even if you can foresee paddling around in your slippersocks for the next 52 ho-hum weekends, don't let Aries suspect it. Your lover needs to be filled with visions of fighting off incredible men who are brighter, richer, taller, tanner and hopelessly in lust with you.

After dating awhile you might want to telephone him on a Sunday morning. Casually ask him to enjoy the beautiful outdoors with you -- "I just feel like being spontaneous today," you say. "Great," he replies half-heartedly, as he pictures a picnic or stroll in the park. Then blow his mind and take him bungie jumping.

Women who play with his mind are also a definite turn off. Aries doesn't like mind games and considers them a total waste of time. If you insist on playing, you may win the battle and find that you've lost the war. That doesn't mean you can't play to win in the eternal game of love, it just means that you have to be subtle.

Remember this important lesson...subtlety, and especially

tact, don't go a long way with Aries, they go *all* the way. That means that even though he's aggressive, your man definitely prefers kid gloves when handling him. Never force feed those lessons you think he should digest.

IS ARIES A ONE WOMAN MAN?

Romantics admire the adventurous spirit of Aries. However, even though we suspect that Columbus was an Aries, we *know* that Houdini was. So while Aries loves the thrill of the chase -- the climb to the top -- too often he performs a disappearing act when he gets bored. And he gets bored very easily. Business deals are dropped after the first challenge fades and the mundane paper work sets in. Do romantic relationships fare any better? Yes, if this restless lover is kept sufficiently on his toes.

Your Ram is capable of being a one-woman man, but only if you're smart enough to furnish him with the variety he loves. Make it part of your agenda to blow the gentleman's mind as often as possible. Surprise him when he least expects it. Live with one foot dangling over the edge. Your interests, your thinking, your whole outlook on life has to provide adrenaline for the Ram.

Yes, it is a full-time job for a very demanding employer -- but if you two have the chemistry to ignite when you unite -- trust Olivia, you will learn to love your work!

DO YOU HAVE WHAT IT TAKES TO SEDUCE ARIES?

It's important to honestly assess your own assets. Just use the mirror of your mind.

Aries needs a woman with vitality and enthusiasm for life. A companion as well as a lover. This ideal partner should have what they call zest in television commercials (the sensation, not the soap)! In France it's called *Joie de vivre* -- the joy of being alive -- and every French woman who made her own history, from Madame Pompadour to Bridgette Bardot, has flaunted it.

Aries knows instinctively that the more active you are, the more alive you feel. These macho lovers consider their bodies high-powered machines and they like their tune-ups in the beautiful outdoors.

Now if your first worry when he asks you to go camping is where in God's name will you plug in your hair dryer, you're not the mate for him. And if you're the type who likes her croissant every morning at 7:15 on the dot..."and why did they put butter on it, they know I never take butter..." well, forget it.

With Aries, if you've done the same thing a dozen times, that's probably ten times too many!

On the other hand, if you're imaginative enough to feed the relationship with a variety of new things to talk about, new sports to try out, new places to explore, new ways to challenge him (and some of these surprises definitely belong in the bedroom) then he may have met his match.

Dynamo Eddie Murphy is a prime example of the aggressive, eye-roving Aries who finally threw away his little black book and settled down. So your erotic mind set should always be to make him believe there's an enigmatic core to you; a part of you that he hasn't as yet penetrated, figuratively speaking.

WHAT COLOR TURNS HIM ON?

You won't find your lover's eyes lighting up at the sight of you in pastel pink with a high lace collar. And did you think that designer dress in granite gray with the steroid shoulder pads would get his juices going? Think again. Taurus may be the sign of the Bull, but it's the Aries man who reacts to the color red like the healthy animal he is. You see, red is the carnal color of passion and its shades will excite your lover to new erotic heights.

Naturally, you can utilize all the hues of the color red in your wardrobe -- from deep, hot pink to lipstick red. Try a red lace teddy, or nightgown or...just a blush?

WHAT'S HIS WORST FAULT?

Every male, at one time or another, has told a woman words that could fertilize Wisconsin. However, Aries has an opposite problem -- diplomacy is not his strong point. Those not in his fan club may call it tactless. Others say he's simply being honest to a fault. One thing is for sure, what's on Aries mind is on his lips -- at exactly the worst moment.

So when you have PMS and the office nerd is celebrating the job you were supposed to get, and your mother is leaving suicidal messages on your answering machine, and your cat just died -- don't, don't, don't ask Aries if you *really* look your age.

DOES HE HAVE A TEMPER?

Aries can flare up like the fourth of July and keep going on and on about it. He can get loud enough to bring the roof down. Then he can get *really* loud. Take comfort in the fact that the phrase "his bark is worse than his bite" was coined for this man.

Avoid direct confrontation with your lover. He can turn militant in a flash and you'll suddenly feel like you're having an affair with George C. Scott playing Patton.

It's true that he has a short memory, so he won't be holding the same old grudge on your second anniversary. But when his temper flares, your Ram can become stubborn. Since he can outshout you anyway, you have to subtly, tactfully, get what you want. Remember?

You know that Aries rules the head, and this sign can be led by the nose if you use a little tact. Always tell your hot-headed lover that he is fine, generous, loyal, loving, understanding -- everything you want him to be -- because he has the power to become all those things.

IS ARIES GOOD WITH CHILDREN?

Yes, Aries loves children and gives of himself willingly. After all, he never lost his childlike love of adventure and thrills, and deep inside is still that little boy who's off to discover Treasure Island.

On the other side of the coin, since Aries is so aggressive himself, he's prone to train his children to be the same way. And when Aries wants something, he wants it *yesterday*. So as his loving mate, it will be your job to convince your husband to let the little tykes reach puberty before expecting them to take over Wall Street.

WHAT DOES ARIES CALL HOME?

Whether it's an apartment or house, your Aries needs his surroundings decorated in strong, magnetic colors. Needless to say, the lipstick-red leather couch that might be too showy for a conservative Capricorn, will be just what ignites the Aries imagination. As for his taste in art, there will probably be bold abstracts on the walls, as opposed to gilt-framed landscapes or pastel watercolors.

The kitchen may show a few cobwebs on the Cuisinart, too. To tell the truth, ask your lover if he has a Cuisinart, and he'll probably tell you that he did until his dermatologist removed it. Chinese take out menus were designed for this man. However, chances are you'll find the latest exercise equipment in the bedroom -- barbells, bicycle, the works. Don't be surprised, either, if you see a mirrored wall or two in this inner sanctum. Your man takes pleasure in watching his body perform the way he wants it to, and that goes for the sight of both of you *performing* together.

Although your lover may not spend as much time at home as a Taurus or Cancer, he does care about how his castle looks. Mainly because it's a reflection of *his* lifestyle, *his* success, *his* image! Aries was the first teacher on how to sell the sizzle and not the steak.

HOW DO YOU DRESS FOR ARIES?

In this area Aries is an old-fashioned fellow. Like his granddaddy, he wants to see Miss Proper with her ankles crossed in the living room, and Madonna with her pouty lips and legs provocatively parted in the bedroom.

No, I am definitely not recommending that you start dressing in black leather and begin carrying a bible -- just dress appropriately for wherever he's taking you. And don't spare the red!

RECIPE FOR A PERFECT EVENING

Delicate crepes are for another evening and another lover. Aries is a meat and potatoes man and loves nothing better than a steak on the rare side and a raw woman on the other side. Of course you're going to eventually get him to cut down on the meat in his diet, but in the meantime, try to cook chicken more than beef and add a few lusty years to his life.

There's another culinary stumbling block: Aries loves variety and this means in his diet, too. He's usually the guest at the wedding reception who hasn't a minute to spend talking, he's too busy working his way through the variety of meatballs and dip.

Actually, Aries runs around so much and relaxes so infrequently, that getting him to sit down and unwind at dinner is a definite accomplishment. But it's really the best thing you can do for his health. Physically and psychologically.

When it comes to keeping his battery energized -- some vitamins and minerals are very important in his diet.

The cell salt for Aries is Potassium Phosphate. It helps to renew the mental strength on which this horny Ram depends. Without it he can become stressed out and cranky. Happily, this cell salt can be found in a wide variety of foods, including cauliflower, spinach, cucumbers, onions, potatoes, olives, apples, bananas, lettuce, walnuts, lentils and lima beans.

Today, with the rise of holistic health practices, we've all become more aware of beneficial herbs. Does your man suffer from headaches? It's a very common complaint among the Rams, whose sign rules the face and head. Cayenne mixed with sage just might relieve it quickly. Blessed Thistle used as a tea will do wonders for your lover's overall health. And when you're cooking, don't be shy with the garlic. It's good for Aries and, as a matter of fact, it's good for everybody. If you really care enough, you might suggest that your lover take *odorless* garlic capsules along with his daily vitamins.

When you finally bring him home with you for that "I did it with my own little hands" fabulous meal, remember that he loves color and light. Place yellow daffodils in a vase, they're an Aries favorite. Then when the scene is set, prepare to whet his appetite for far more than food...

FIRST STEP

Since this recipe is Italian, Olivia suggests that you go all out on decorating. Set the romantic mood with a red checkered tablecloth and candles dripping color down the sides of Chianti bottles. It's a lot of fun for a few lire.

As for what you'll wear, why not carry out the scenario just a little further? A romantic white silk poet's shirt with scooped neckline and long flowing sleeves. Wear it with a long black skirt or black silk pants. For music, I'd love to suggest that you hire a little old Italian man to stand in the corner serenading

you on the violin, but I'll rein in my imagination and settle for a
bluesy sax on the stereo.

Pour a red Italian wine. Chianti will do just fine, or something more expensive if you more than like him. Then serve the
salad. Make sure to prepare it well enough in advance so that it
will be cold and crisp.

SECOND STEP: SINFUL SALAD

1 clove garlic
1/4 cup olive oil
1/2 tsp salt
1/2 tsp pepper
1 tbs. white wine vinegar
1 head of iceberg or romaine lettuce
2 tomatoes cut up
1/2 cucumber, sliced
2 radishes, sliced
1/4 green pepper cut up into small pieces.
Anchovy optional

In the Italian manner, rub the crushed garlic pieces over the
inside of the salad bowl. Mix the oil, salt, pepper, and vinegar.
Place it all in a bowl with lettuce. Don't bother adding Italian
dressing until you are ready to serve. Mix very well.

THIRD STEP: GARLIC BREAD APHRODISIAC:

Serve this crisp, delicious salad with garlic bread: You'll need
one loaf of Italian or French bread. Three cloves of garlic. Cut it
into one inch slices, cover with butter and sprinkle with garlic
powder, salt and pepper, mince garlic cloves and distribute
evenly, before toasting or baking for fifteen minutes or until
golden brown. Mmmmm, nothing smells as wonderful!

INTERMISSION:

By now, your Aries lover has loosened his belt and has the
look of a very contented cat.

Let him sip his wine and listen to the stereo (treat him to Elton John, another Aries, or if you're lucky enough to have found a lover of classical music, Bach was yet another Aries soulmate). Then, when he's lost in the music, it's time for you to slip into the kitchen and remove the highlight of the meal from the oven

FOURTH STEP: POLLO DE PASSION

3 & 1/2 pound chicken, cut up
3   tablespoons olive oil
14 olives, half green, half black
2 cloves of minced garlic
1   carrot minced
1   small tomato diced
1   onion minced
1   green pepper diced
2   cups chicken bouillon
4   tbs. tomato sauce.
1/2 cup dry white wine
pinch oregano
Pepper to taste

Note: It's not necessary to add salt to this dish, the olives provide all you need.

Pour the olive oil into a skillet and lightly brown chicken and garlic. Add the wine, tomato, carrots, green pepper and onion. When the onion is lightly browned, add the two cups of chicken bouillon. Cut up five olives, mash the pulp of five olives and add to stock. Put in the rest of the olives whole. Add tomato sauce and simmer 30 to 40 minutes until the sauce is nice and thick.

Don't forget to keep his wine glass filled.

INTERMISSION #2:

It takes place about an hour later, while you're both relaxing in the living room. Since your Aries may be feeling a little sleepy at this point, it's the perfect time to bring in coffee and dessert.

FIFTH STEP: SENSUAL STRAWBERRIES

After you wash the strawberries, sprinkle with a little sugar and pour Marsala over them. If you don't have Marsala, a sweet red wine will do just as well. Mix and chill in the refrigerator until ready to serve.

The finest way to serve your *coup d' amour* is to put some strawberries in a pretty dessert dish or champagne glass. Then top it all with whipped cream. If you really want to be decadent, put the strawberries in the dish, a scoop of chocolate pudding over that and the whipped cream on top of it all. One plump strawberry nestled in the whipped cream is the finishing touch.

WHAT'S THE MOST SENSITIVE PART OF HIS BODY?

Aries rules the head (he might even have a telltale scar or birthmark on some part of his head or face) and when under stress your lover has been known to suffer from simple headaches to severe migraines. Since you don't want to find yourself with a roommate who whines: "Not tonight, darling, I have a headache," the best medicine is to welcome him home from whatever war he's fighting with a soothing, cool hand upon his brow. Your other hand can welcome him too...a *memorable* homecoming that's been known to work quicker than aspirin!

Now lower the lights and raise the music level.

Scent your fingertips with your own special fragrance (or with a touch of ginger, his magic scent) and have him lie on the sofa with his head nestled in your lap. Gently begin stroking his temples and work from the back of his neck up to where those nasty knots are tied. Run your thumbs over his eyelids, pressing ever so gently. Ah, that moan tells you that he likes it. Increase the pressure a little more. Use your index fingers in a circular motion to lightly massage his temples. Although his symbol is the Ram, macho Aries will purr like a pussycat.

Of course, it won't be long before he'll want to change places with you. Remember, it was probably Aries who invented the missionary position for its sense of control and power (not to mention that with his low threshold for repetition, he could leave whenever things got boring)!

WHERE IS THAT ROMANTIC GETAWAY?

You've given Aries that wonderful water-proof jacket for white water rafting on his birthday. Or, perhaps goggles for his red race car. Or a racquetball for his lunch time macho-chism. Now it follows that the perfect escape will offer him a chance to enjoy them.

Better yet, share the adventure with him. Of course that means that you could end up sharing all the fun of mosquitoes in a tent the salesman *swore* would be water proof, etc. etc.

Just how much do you love this man?

Germany is ruled by Aries, so if you have the money or if your Aries lover likes spending lots of his, think about foreign excitement. The Ram's idea of heaven is trekking over the Alps and making wild, passionate love in-between peaks. Who can resist a man who is turned on by a little danger on his vacation and in his woman!

Of course, if you want to stay closer to home, it's easy enough to find plenty of beautiful mountains and inns that are never too far away from major airports.

But on second thought...did I say, sleeping in a tent? In the beautiful outdoors?

Imagine the setting: the two of you hidden in some mountain retreat, surrounded by primitive sounds of the night. He lights a fire and when he kisses you the sparks of passion fly...soon his bronze, muscular body is gleaming in the glow of the coals...the flames are reflected in the intensity of his eyes...you take his handsome head in your hands and draw him down beside you into the soft grass...and...and...damn, now that's what Olivia calls a vacation!

HOW TO PLEASE ARIES SEXUALLY.

Lets begin with you in a short cloth robe as you step from a hot, steamy shower. Your skin is beautifully flushed, legs as smooth as a quick depilatory can make them (and you remembered to put on body oil while your skin was slightly moist). Now, with your hair freshly shampooed and only towel-dried, you come out of the bathroom and into the bedroom, barefoot. The lights have been turned down and just candlelight glows. The effect is to have you beautifully backlit from the bathroom.

You walk over to where your lover is sitting in a chair. (Yes, you *specifically* asked him to wait for you there.)

The erotic game begins....

Of course, his fantasies about what you had in mind when you asked him to wait until you showered, has already driven him crazy. He didn't realize it of course, but the moment you took control and had him agree to wait for you in that chair... that was the moment the seduction began.

We don't want macho Aries to lie down on the bed...*not yet*. If he should speak, just raise your finger to your lips to signal that you prefer he remain quiet.

A walk on the wild side....

Now, slowly walk to the foot of the bed and, positioning your body slightly sideways, bend over and reach down to where you placed a pair of spiked black pumps.

(Not bending your knees wins you 10 erotic points.)

Please don't go saying this is corny and that you would be too embarrassed doing it. There is nothing cliché about sexual glamour and "turn-ons" that have been time-proven. Beautiful legs in sexy spikes are an eternal turn-on. Bending over is also a lovely way to treat Aries to the back line of your leg and calf, and the softly lit curve of your bottom. His first thought will be to kiss what he sees. His second thought will be to spank it. His final thought will be which he wants first.

Then, sit down, crossing ankle over knee and slip on the first shoe. At this point, your Aries lover should be mesmerized, eagerly awaiting your next move -- which is to switch legs and slowly put on the other shoe. You can recreate that classic scene in the film "Basic Instinct" and give him a view of heaven (as you deliberately raise your knees when crossing your legs), but that's up to how naughty you feel. Or how generous.

It is very important that you never take your eyes off his eyes.

Practicing this erotic choreography in front of a full-length mirror is not only allowed but encouraged. Do it until you have a true sensual rhythm and you can pull it off without giggling -- and that means *concentration on the act.*

Remember, Olivia told you at the start that when it came to the five senses, the mind makes the most sense. You are now beginning to understand that this is the most erotic lesson of all.

Walk slowly toward him until you are within touching distance and, with one hand, *slightly* untie the belt on your robe, not enough to open it, but just enough to hand him the loosened belt. It's hard to imagine aggressive Aries becoming so shaken at this point that he won't know what to do with that soft rope you're handing him, but just in case your lover is temporarily stunned, take his hand gently and wrap the end of the belt around it.

An erotic power play...

There is no power equal to that of a beautiful woman standing before her lover in high heels, her gown slightly open, her skin glowing in candlelight, perfumed oil on her warm, naked body. Naturally, you are standing perfectly straight, your body language promising "I am your equal." This unspoken message, along with the intense visuals, will arouse Aries, who doesn't only adore a challenge, but whose very nature demands one.

If it takes him longer than three seconds to reach up and grab that robe, then *slowly, ever so slowly,* with your shoulders back, and your eyes never leaving his, allow it slip to the floor.

At this point, seeing your fragile vulnerability, your lover will want to assert himself and take control. Of course, the possibilities are endless, but here are three erotic scenarios.

For the Aries who thinks of you as "his little girl" -- he might pull you down on his lap. Or, the control-freak lover, whose favorite movie is '9 1/2', might want to see you strut around the room in those spiked heels. But if your lover is instinctively erotic, he will place his hands gently on your hips and slowly turn you around until you have come full circle. Whatever fate deals you at this stage, I promise it will be very exciting.

Actually, chances are that Aries is so hot at this point, that if he's not experienced in erotica he might want to hurry things up. Calmly quiet him and refuse to let this happen. It's part of the game. Take control and keep him in the chair. It's up to your lover to figure out how to take back that control.

Note: The above scenario demands that you wear nothing under your robe. However, since some of us are less blessed than others (you Jane Fonda dropouts know who you are), if you absolutely must, a pair of lace bikini panties or even a red

lace teddy can be worn. But the effect is far more devastating if
you have the imagination and courage to go for the gold.

Put yourself in his hands...

Now, do not sit on his lap at this point, but stand next to him
and quietly, gracefully, bend over and lie submissively across
his lap. You don't have to say a word. It is the ultimate, excruci-
atingly sexy posture for Aries. He now has his options of what
to do with that masculine right or left hand, depending on
which way you face.

He may decide on his *second* thought.

If he does, he'll use words to set up the scenario. No doubt
having a lot to do with your being a very naughty girl to tease
him this way.

If you've never been spanked, the first thing you have to
know is that more women than Madonna like hanky-spanky.
Needless to say, but I'll say it anyway, you're not in this intimate situation with someone you just met at a produce counter.
Take this very important advice from Olivia and *never* expose
yourself (pun unintended) to possible violence. It takes trust
and knowing someone long enough to play out a sexual fantasy
like this. Also, it makes sense that you should be totally relaxed
and trusting with someone in order to have fun with the game.

Now you may usually be very aggressive and find it hard to
imagine yourself in such a submissive role. But let's remember
our goal -- *to seduce Aries heart, mind, body and soul*. Your
man has a need for control and to have you submit lovingly and
adoringly. (The latter is icing on the Ram's cake.) I'm not saying
that later on in the relationship you can't play out some of your
more dominant traits, like undressing *him*, but right now, try
the above scenario, you will probably love it.

From this point on, life will move to its own rhythms.

Share the fantasy...

Of course, once you have established an on-going sexual relationship with Aries, it's important to remember how provocative the other side of the coin can be.

In just the same way as Aries loves control, he gets turned on
fantasizing about being submissive to a woman. That's why silk
scarves are used in better erotic films to bind wrists. If you
missed that exciting foreign film in which a silk scarf, knotted

at every inch, was inserted into the lover's bottom until just the end could be held, only to be slowly withdrawn as he climaxed, until he went out of his mind...don't wait for his birthday before you surprise him.

A future turn-on that is irresistible to your lover is to have sex in public. You can ease into this gently by turning off all the lights in the bedroom or hotel room where you're making love and opening the blinds to the mysterious, ever peeking night. If the air is warm, raise the windows. It's lovely to feel the balmy breeze on your skin -- and deliciously erotic, too.

In time, you can expand this to beaches, airplane bathrooms, etc. As for the latter, it isn't just a comedian's joke -- many lovers give it a try because it's very high excitement. How quickly can you have an orgasm? Can you keep the stewardess out? Can you get away with it? Aries will love to try. Best of all, he'll love the fact that you would be adventurous enough, and hot enough, to do it. However, if you're the type of lover who needs an hour's foreplay... well, you may want to take a train.

Arise and arouse...

Sex with passionate Aries is wonderful at any hour, but don't forget that your lover is especially responsive before he goes off to fight his war in the schoolroom, boardroom or mailroom. That means love in the early morning. Get up a little before you wake him and slip into the bathroom. Brushing your teeth and getting all those pedestrian necessities out of the way will make the thought of sex more appealing.

Crawl back under the warm covers. Don't be surprised if when you reach for your lover he's already early-morning-hard. Then gently stroke him, hardly touching him, till your fingers acquire a sensitivity that lets you feel the velvet of his skin -- touching him so lightly that you're leaving room for the electricity to move between your flesh and his.

That spark is chemistry.

Remember, you can't be in a hurry. That means a practice session with a fuzzy peach (bananas are too smooth). You want to close your eyes and run your fingers softly around the peach until the tips of your fingers can discern the fuzz only.

You caress your lover in this erotic manner until he begins to move his body. With Aries, you're not in for a long wait. Don't stop until you get him to moan and squirm. It's delicious torture.

If he wakes up and takes control, that's fine. If he keeps his eyes closed, then perhaps he wants the other side of that coin again -- to let *you* play director. The typical Aries male fantasy of being the little boy who is awakened in the morning, before he goes to school, by a female figure who "makes him do things under the covers."

Remember once more that you always begin to make love slowly, trying to involve all your senses...concentrating on how he smells, feels, looks, sounds. Only until you lose yourself in your Aries lover will you find the erotic bliss you have always desired.

TAURUS

APR 20 – MAY 20

RULING PLANET: VENUS

FEMININE, NEGATIVE, EARTH SIGN

EROTIC DRIVE: TO POSSESS

COLOR: GREEN

PASSION FLOWER: MARIGOLD

MAGICAL SCENT: VERBENA

GEM: EMERALD

METAL: COPPER

HERBS:

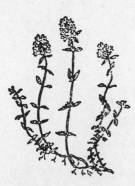

Thyme　　　　Tansy　　　　Heather

"And she, slow, patient, draws him to her
and starts to undress him, with her eyes
shut. Slowly, he makes as if to help her.
She tells him to keep still."
Marguerite Duras, "The Lover"

Here is the bull with all his strength, stubbornness and sensuality. Taurus is ruled by Venus, the planet of love and beauty, so your man is probably better than average looking. Valentino was the ultimate erotic Taurus. We don't have to hear his voice in those old movies to imagine what an intense lover he was. Sometimes Venus bestows dimples on these men, giving them an even greater advantage.

Since Taurus is an earth sign, chances are that he has both feet on the ground. The only problem is that sometimes he can dig those heels too deeply into the earth and get stuck in the proverbial rut.

To begin with, don't become involved with this man if you want someone full of surprises. Taureans like their routine and it takes a lot of maneuvering, not to mention occasional sticks of dynamite to change their direction.

On the positive side, your Taurus is ruled by Venus, and oh, does he love the art of love! The Bull is sexually demanding and his drive can reach marathon proportions. If you haven't as yet felt the need for mega vitamins, this lover may just convince you.

Whereas Aries might take the initiative and make the first move, Taurus is more practical. He prefers to shop before he buys. No, he isn't looking for a bargain, just for the best quality woman on the market. Besides, he intends to be around to celebrate his 50th wedding anniversary, so he wants to be as sure of his emotional investment as possible.

Since friendships are an important part of his life, it's possible that you'll find yourself his friend long before you're his lover, and that's a wonderful way to begin an affair. As Dustin

Hoffman told Jessica Lang at the end of "Tootsie" -- "The hard part's over, we're already good friends."

Once you are lovers though, it is vital to bring a little sexual experimentation into the Bull's life. Olivia has warned you that Taurus isn't apt to change his ways, so if you don't want to be memorizing the patterns on your ceiling for the next ten years, you'd better take this man in hand. Yes, I mean it *exactly* that way. Actually, just keep reading and you will learn all the erotic pleasures your mama never taught you.

WHAT TURNS HIM ON?

Taureans are nurturing and protective. They envision a perfect world where an adoring wife, obedient children, faithful friend, and fleas, adorable pet (who never once soils the carpet) surround them in perfect harmony. Therefore, take the time to make yourself and your home beautiful for your own Taurus -- a warm and safe nest where he can always find peace.

The first chance you may get to show off your hideaway is when you invite him *chez vous* for dinner. More on that momentous occasion later. However, suffice it to say right now that if you lack a little skill in the kitchen (guests eat your mashed potatoes with knife and fork?) it would be wise to pick up a few cookbooks and start practicing. The last thing your lover wants is a woman who eats out every night, or thinks that adding thyme to Hamburger Helper is a gourmet experience.

Also, Taurus has a tendency to preach a little and an attentive -- make that transfixed -- ear from you will be very appreciated. So while he's rambling on about the joys of French cooking or whatever, listen with rapt attention.

Last but not least, be the type of lover who doesn't save her sensual ways for the bedroom only. That means give your Bull a lot of affectionate hugs. He's the hugging, loving, stroking kind, and he gives as good as he gets.

WHAT TURNS HIM OFF?

Lectures from you, no matter how well meaning. If you want to get your point across to a Taurus lover, then step down from the lectern and speak lovingly, sweetly, or, as they say in Brooklyn, *forgeddaboudit!*

Remember too, that his sense of security is all important. If he sees you giving the eye in too many directions, he'll get cold feet and cold feet definitely do not a warm heart make. Taurus has to feel that you're dependable...that you'll be there for him.

This man works hard for his money. Sometimes the less evolved type can love it even more than sex with you (yes, I'm talking serious lust here), and the last thing he wants is a woman who doesn't respect the value of his dollar. So if you get an urge every now and then to spend money like it's water -- dip into your own well.

Another Taurean turn-off is a woman who likes to rearrange his furniture. His *things* are sacred to him because they give him a much needed sense of security. They are extensions of his very self. Your man likes his favorite objects *just the way they are*, and keep your pretty hands off his favorite cushion that's on his favorite chair, next to his favorite lamp, but thanks for the thought.

In the same way that he hates radical changes in furniture arrangement, just try serving white wine instead of his beloved red (or visa versa) and he'll become as disoriented as if you slipped LSD into his mouthwash.

Still hanging in there?

IS TAURUS A ONE WOMAN MAN?

If the relationship is a happy one sexually, yes. However, even if trouble occurs, his stubbornness works in your favor, because he'll hang in there long after you've thrown in your Her towel. He can be wounded by arguments, suffering from being ignored and dying from jealousy -- but he won't give up while there's a drop of life left in him. He loves you, it's as simple as that. The constant love of a Taurus can sustain both of you through emotional fires and floods.

Also, as you now know, your lover is a man who hates change. All these factors will keep him working overtime to make everything right.

DO YOU HAVE WHAT IT TAKES TO SEDUCE TAURUS?

You don't have to be gorgeous like Farrah Fawcett to seduce a

famous Bull like Ryan O'Neal. However, you do have to have
your act together. For instance, how mature are you? No, I don't
mean in years. It's just that Taurus needs someone he can count
on, someone who's ready to settle down.

The most wonderful gift you can give this man is *old-fashioned fidelity*. Just think of it, having someone who will be
devoted to you and only you. In return, you must give him the
one-on-one attention that he craves.

Are you grown up enough to do it? Or are you the girl who
loves to "cruise" parties, looking for validation from every male
that you're the sexiest thing in the room? Hopefully, you already
know who you are and what a prize you've won in the Bull --
because once he knows that you're committed in the deepest
sense, then Taurus can relax and begin to really love you back.

WHAT COLOR TURNS HIM ON?

Green, as in the color of money, of course. Although Taurus
does have a strong affinity for the power and luxuries money
brings, never forget that beauty is very important to him, too.
Like Libra he is Venus-ruled and that means his sense of aesthetics is high toned. The time you take to look gorgeous for
him is never wasted.

Have a lot of nature's greenery in your home, too. Nothing
makes living more comfortable or serene than being surrounded
by beautiful plants -- in all their hues from lime to emerald
green. It will help to create the oasis of peace that your lover
will be eager to call *home.*

WHAT'S HIS WORST FAULT?

If you're very spiritual, then you might be put off by his love
of money and material things. Remember though why they're so
important to him -- because Taurus needs this sense of identity
reflected through the things he owns. However, he doesn't have
a stingy bone in his beautiful body, and that can more than
make up for it.

If you've got a mind of your own and then some, you might
not like how didactic the Bull can be. What's an example? Just
refute which wine goes with what foods and listen to him out-
pontificate the Pontiff!

Happily, Taurus has a great sense of humor (he's a natural mimic) so if he becomes a little pompous from time to time, just cool off and then kindly show him how dumb it all was. He usually gets the joke, even when it's on him.

Oh yes, Taurus can be possessive and that can be a turn off to independent females. Remember that it's only because he has a fear of losing you. It's the same fear that makes him acquire *things* -- the Mercedes, the stereo, the wall-to-wall television -- possessing luxuries make this poor baby feel more secure.

It's a strange malady, and TLC is the only known cure.

DOES HE HAVE A BAD TEMPER?

What's interesting about this man are layers of complicated emotions that lie beneath the surface. Yes, he's easy going enough, but he has a fiery temper (you've heard of the Raging Bull?) and he doesn't forgive or forget an insult. So watch your tongue, but *only* when speaking, that is.

IS TAURUS GOOD WITH CHILDREN?

Yes, Taurus makes a great daddy, but he does tend to be too easy.

On the other hand, he likes his children to be disciplined with a set routine. If the little tykes, or big tykes for that matter, deviate from their set routine too often, daddy gets nervous. It's a matter of "I like life this way, so why don't you?" Taurus has to learn to give his children the freedom to be themselves.

WHAT DOES TAURUS CALL HOME?

No man's castle was ever treated more royally than his. Taureans consider home their haven, their escape, their nest, their own place and don't you ever forget it.

Chances are the furniture in your lover's home is big and comfortable. A sofa he can sink into with big oversized pillows. This is one fellow who definitely won't unwind at the end of a rough day in a dainty Queen's Anne's chair. The bed will be king-size and if he has the money to install a large Jacuzzi in the bathroom, it will be there, too.

There's quality art work on the walls and the kitchen is a cook's dream, stocked with every herb and the latest model everything. If it cuts, chops, mashes, or purees, Taurus will have two of them. So if you're searching for the perfect gift for his birthday, you can never go wrong choosing something to make his home (concentrate on the kitchen) even more appealing.

If he has the money and the time...the whole effect of his abode will be ultra inviting and sensual.

HOW DO YOU DRESS FOR TAURUS?

Frame your face in a lace collar with grandmother's brooch at your throat. Oh, granny wore black leather? Well, then you can always hunt for a brooch in an antique shop. A feminine old-fashioned touch on a sheer, definitely nineties blouse, will go right to the heart of this sentimental lover. Then, just as you're going out the door, whisper in his ear that you're a little chilly, and it must be your barely-there French bikini underwear. His imagination should have him racing through dessert and shouting shortcuts at the taxi driver.

Remember always that your Bull loves the good things of life -- and that means fine clothing, too -- rich fabrics, particularly silks, and good design. Elegant, subtle taste will always win his shrewd approval.

RECIPE FOR A PERFECT EVENING

You probably have the idea by now that food is *very* important to Taureans -- and I mean the look of it, the preparation, and the way you serve it. The intimate dinner that you plan should be given *great* attention. You can count on Taurus giving equal attention to the wine he brings.

Because your lover prefers sumptuous meals, sometimes that preference begins to show around his middle. There will be more time later on to get him exercising -- now is the time to seduce and spoil him. Make the dining area (even if it's ten feet of kitchen) as attractive as possible: best dishes, candles, etc. If you think about putting out plastic placemats, think again. Ketchup bottle on the table? Do you want to live through dessert?

Oh yes, music should be playing romantically in the background. Some mellow La Streisand, another Taurus, will do fine.

Most likely, the man's a great cook himself (you just can't love food as much as Taurus without knowing how to put it together). But don't be intimidated. He'll love to teach you his secret spaghetti sauce. Think of all the wonderfully sensual finger licking it involves. If you know your way around a cutting board, all the better, it will be mutual admiration time.

His cell salt is Sulphate of Soda which keeps the body's supply of water in balance. Note for future meals: some foods especially good for the Bull's health are beets, cabbage, cauliflower, onion and pumpkin.

Using beneficial herbs should be part of your daily life, whether you're madly in love or not. Nothing is sadder than the female who dreams of finding that powerful lover but neglects her own health; so when she finally finds him, she can't keep up with him!

Now, since you've taken the time to find out your lover's favorite foods, I'll tell you what herbs are good for him.

Sage and thyme are important. Taurus rules the throat, remember? That means he's prone to strep throats, flu and so on. Sage is very good for his throat, and try using it as a tea also.

Start the meal off with a salad, because these greens, along with the kind you deposit, are a big favorite with Taurus.

Remember that I said your lover is most comfortable when dining elegantly? Well, I don't expect you to duplicate the crystal at the Plaza, but take care to have a pretty tablecloth or mats, with cloth napkins, candles, etc. Elegance doesn't require a lot of money, but taste, imagination and planning are essential. It's simply atmosphere -- what they call ambiance in overpriced French restaurants.

As for the final decoration -- yourself -- wear something green with a neckline that will widen his pupils when you lean over to toss the salad.

FIRST STEP: CARESSING CAESAR SALAD

1 head of Romaine lettuce
1/4 cup lemon juice
1/2 tsp Worcestershire sauce
1/2 tsp dry mustard
1/2 tsp garlic salt
1/4 tsp pepper
2 1/2 tsp grated Parmesan cheese
1 egg.

Break the lettuce into salad bowl in bite size pieces. Put in the refrigerator for just about an hour. Combine lemon juice, Worcestershire sauce, mustard, garlic salt and pepper and pour over greens. Sprinkle with cheese. Break the egg over it all. Toss gently until all the leaves are coated and the egg completely disappears. Sprinkle with crumbled bacon, if you like finishing touches, and serve as your first course.

Note: After the salad, impress Taurus by serving him a little sherbet (sorbet to those who shop in gourmet markets). If he knows his gourmet rituals, he'll recognize that sherbert is served to freshen the palate between courses. If he just thinks it's an off-the-wall, goofy way to serve ice-cream, that's okay, too.

SECOND STEP: LASCIVIOUS LASAGNE

1 cup minced onion
1 tbs. vegetable oil
1 pound ground turkey
1 clove minced garlic
1/4 cup diced green pepper
1 tsp. salt
1 tsp. pepper
1 tsp. dry mustard
1/4 tsp. oregano
3 tsp. minced parsley
1/4 tsp. basil
2 1/2 cups canned tomatoes

1 can (8 oz) tomato sauce
1/2 cup grated Parmesan cheese
8 ounces Lasagne or wide noodles
1 pound ricotta cheese
3/4 cup thinly sliced mozzarella cheese

Sauté the onions in oil until lightly browned and then add
the ground turkey. Cook for about four minutes or until the red-
ness is gone.

Combine garlic and all the spices, along with green pepper,
tomatoes, tomato sauce and 1/4 cup Parmesan cheese. Simmer
with the meat mixture for about 45 minutes.

Cook pasta according to directions on the package. Drain and
rinse in cold water.

Heat oven to 350 F. and place 1/3 of meat sauce in a 3-quart
baking dish. Cover with a layer of Lasagne placed lengthwise.
Then place a layer of Mozzarella, followed by a layer of ricotta,
sprinkle with 1/4 cup of Parmesan cheese. Bake about 30 minutes.

THIRD STEP: CARNAL CAULIFLOWER

Although the Lasagne is substantial enough to satisfy the
healthiest appetite, you never know with Taurus. This man seriously likes to eat. So I suggest that you serve a vegetable just to
be on the safe side.

1 small cauliflower
1 1/2 cups of sour cream sauce (Just add garlic and spices)
2 tbs grated Parmesan cheese
1 1/2 tbs bread crumbs
1/4 cup butter

Break off the flowerets and boil in salted water about 10 minutes. Drain and place in buttered baking dish. Cover with the
cream sauce, sprinkle with cheese and bread crumbs and dot
with butter. Bake in hot oven (400 F) about 20 minutes.

You can put this dish in the oven for the last 20 minutes with
the Lasagne.

Note: Serve this meal with accompanying rose or burgundy
wine. *Don't save pennies on the wine.* This is one area where

your lover knows his vineyards, and he'll appreciate a finer choice.

INTERMISSION:

While coffee is brewing, take yourself, your Taurus and your wine into the living room. If you didn't know that your man appreciates good art, from the old masters to the new, be aware of it now. That means your tacky blue period Picasso print (the one you've had since college) has got to go. The same for the chipped plaster bust of Nefertiti. If you don't have the budget to put oils, watercolors or pastels on your walls, how about some interesting, well-framed photography?

Your Bull should be feeling well sated now and in the mood to talk. Give him enough time to relax and digest that rich meal before totally spoiling him. Since a typical Taurus is never really happy until his sweet tooth is satisfied...

FIFTH STEP: SINFUL CHOCOLATE CAKE

A Hollywood starlet who knew what she was talking about, once said: "Give a man mouth-watering chocolate cake and he'll give you *anything.*"

Make the coffee strong and the chocolate cake as gooey, rich and deliciously sinful as possible. Taurus may be a little shy in asking, so suggest "would you like a scoop of chocolate ice cream on that cake?"

Yes, it's a low trick, but in seducing a lover, heart, mind, body and soul...have no shame!

Note: Make this dinner for a Saturday night so that your lover can work off all those pounds on a Sunday hike. If hiking sounds too radical, then at least walk around the park. Your Bull has a tendency to overeat, and he'll need your encouragement in staying fit.

WHAT'S THE MOST SENSITIVE PART OF HIS BODY?

Taurus rules the neck and throat and many singers (including Ella Fitzgerald and Stevie Wonder) are Taureans. When he final-

ly relaxes enough to hum a little Billy Joel in your ear, you'll
know your man feels really fine. Just think of what great shower
duets the future holds.

As you gently rub the day's worries from the back of his neck,
finish with little kisses and gentle nibbles up and down this
most sensitive area. It should have Taurus pleading for mercy,
and if you really care, you won't give him a drop.

Of course, this also means that Taurus is prone to sore throats
(we hope he doesn't smoke). I can't resist this wonderfully
corny old joke:

"My date asked me if I smoked after making love. I don't
know, I said, I never looked!"

It's important to keep a supply of herbal teas on hand to
soothe his throat if it gets scratchy. When Christmas or his birthday comes around, give him a lovely cashmere scarf to nestle
against his neck. Everytime he feels its silky softness he'll think
of the more intimate parts of you.

WHERE IS THAT ROMANTIC GETAWAY?

Taurus is an earth sign and he doesn't like being too far away
from the beauty of the lady he loves most -- Mother Nature.

He unwinds in the country and a charming inn nestled in
Ireland (a Taurus-ruled country) would be ideal. However, since
that price tag may be a bit high, there's nothing wrong with
domestic grass either. Choose your favorite away-from-it-all spot
and then select a really charming inn. Remember that your
Taurus likes to go first class, so save your pennies and do it
right!

Picnics by bubbling streams, the hot sun on your neck as you
lean provocatively forward (in your soft white peasant blouse,
of course). You dip your finger into the pate and lick it off very
slowly, never taking your eyes from his.

Later you read him poetry (Robert Browning was a famed
romantic Taurus)...until his hand on your thigh makes your
voice weak. And then, much later...the smell of those crisp
country linens on your fluffy feather bed at night...the hypnotic
sound of crickets...the utter stillness except for his breathing
mingling with your own...the lowering of the oil lamp...the...

HOW TO PLEASE TAURUS SEXUALLY.

You've been touching each other and kissing and holding and caressing...and you're both very hot. Your lover is quickly moving into third gear. It's time to extend the passion while you seduce his heart, mind and soul...as well as his body.

"In any good game of sport," you whisper in his ear, "when the player gets overheated, they send him to the showers."

Then take his hand and lead him into the bathroom.

Steam heat ..

You've already made sure that all bath oils and powders are placed strategically in the bedroom and bathroom so that you won't have to hunt for them later.

Also, take a cold, clinical look at the shower curtain, bath mat and towels, if they're a little ragged around the edges, mark it on your shopping list to replace them. Everything should be pleasingly fresh, soft and sexy.

I firmly believe that if there's ever a time a girl should be her own best friend, it's when she's about to stand naked in the bathroom. So definitely use just one red light in the bathroom instead of the standard fluorescent that shows no mercy.

Now as you turn on the shower, be aware that every moment he's watching you. That means that you hold your stomach in and keep your breasts high, and when you bend over, you don't so much bend as perform a sensual ballet movement...one that shows the beautiful lines of your body. If you skipped ballet lessons and opted for piano, then graceful kneeling will do.

Let the sound of the water and the steam build up as you carefully remove any clothing or jewelry from both of you. As you do this, give him a prelude of what's to come by lightly kissing his throat up and down...slowly, erotically. This is a very erogenous area for Taurus and he'll feel it down to his toes.

A wet dream...

How do you wash your lover in the shower? You begin by telling him that you're going to treat him like a baby and that's why you have that big, white creamy bar of Ivory. Then you take your huge, fluffy, natural sea sponge and soap it up. Squeeze it until it bubbles.

Starting at his shoulders, run the sponge across his back, then slowly soap up his entire body until he looks dipped in a silky foam. What do you do about his genitals? You pay *them* extra attention, of course. You might even want to put aside the sponge at this point and let your fingers caress and clean this delicious area. Don't forget to lovingly polish all the equipment. At this point, hand your lover the sponge and let him soap you up. Isn't the sensation wonderful? By the time you're ready to rinse off, there should be more steam coming from both of you than from the shower.

If your shaky knees will allow it, step out of the shower and into those big fluffy bath towels. Use one to dry your hair and to pat yourself lightly, but that's all. Both of you should go back to the bedroom wet, damp, moist, slightly dripping and...feeling the chill in the evaporation.

Before you get into bed, switch on that two hour tape you made from the most erotic love songs in your CD collection. That insures that mood will be just right and that no unexpected country western will jar it. For those of you who find country western highly erotic, play on!

Forbidden fruit...

I'm going to whisper a little secret about your lover: he likes to masturbate while he fantasizes. Perhaps he's never done this in front of a woman, but you can bet this erotic image has been in his dreams.

Next to the bed is the massage oil. Pour some in the palm of your hand. Slowly, slowly, slowly, caress his penis with the warm oil until he moves in exquisite agony. Then take his other hand and slowly, slowly, slowly put it on his sex...while you keep kissing him. If he takes his hand away, you don't exactly have to call a taxi, but this lover has a long way to go in learning how to please you and himself.

If you're still interested and you think this Taurus lover is worth educating, urge him to keep caressing himself. Place your oiled hands under his bottom where you can lift him, telling him to stretch his legs. Your mouth is on his throat, kissing, licking it...gently biting...as his body reaches up...and he reaches the point of no return.

Then, back to the showers.

I promise that Taurus will be so appreciative of this erotic trip that you've taken him on, that he will soon be ready (remember, he has all that wonderful energy of the bull) to give you his full loving attention.

Note: Nothing makes our mouths dryer than the fire our bodies create when making love. Therefore, along with candles in
the bedroom, always have cool drinks or fruit within reach of
the bed.

Your mouth may be much too busy to enjoy them during your
erotic lovemaking...but perhaps in-between acts?

Share the fantasy...

In the future, you might want to fulfill another erotic fantasy
of Taurus, and actually have that picnic. Only this time the spot
you find will be very, very secluded and you will eat and make
love...and eat and make more love...and not necessarily in that
order.

Just make sure that you put the ketchup where the ketchup
belongs!

GEMINI

MAY 21 – JUNE 21

RULING PLANET: MERCURY

MASCULINE, POSITIVE, AIR SIGN

EROTIC DRIVE: TO FANTASIZE

COLOR: YELLOW

GEM: AGATE

PASSION FLOWER: FREESIA

MAGICAL SCENT: ALMOND

METAL: MERCURY

HERBS:

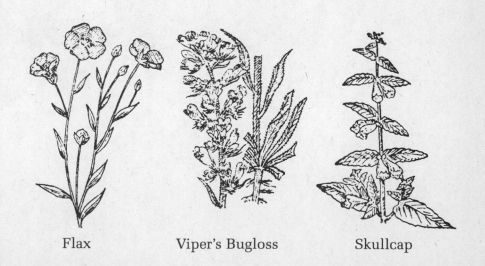

Flax   Viper's Bugloss   Skullcap

**"They ain't never gonna love you any
better babe. And they nee-eever gonna
love you right. So you better dig it
right now, right now."**

                                        **Janis Joplin,
                                        "Kozmic Blues"**

They say that when you fall in love your head is in the
clouds, and I think that's a perfect place for loving this fascinating air sign.

Ruled by the planet Mercury, your Gemini is a more cerebral
kind of lover -- he listens to his mind before his heart -- and his
mind is always working, planning, calculating, scheming and
dreaming.

Gemini is a born communicator -- verbally and with the written word. Many a writer is born under this sign (Herman Woulk
is one, Arthur Miller another) and you can look forward to
receiving fascinating letters, full of wit, and often full of more
promise than Gemini delivers. A few past lovers might say that
most of the air in this air sign is hot. Ouch!

It's just that Gemini is a true master at orchestrating words
and moods -- and sometimes romantic phrases roll off his
tongue quicker than his emotions can keep up. Add to the con-
fusing mix Gemini's symbol -- the Twins (he's always got two
things going at once) -- and take what you hear with the proverbial bushels of salt.

Of course this charmer means his sweet words at the moment,
but just wait a minute -- make that a second -- Gemini might
just change his mind. This is the fellow who might suddenly
decide to take off to the races only to get itchy feet and head for
a round-trip spree in London. So you see, until he really com-
mits, nothing is for sure.

Being a Mercury-ruled baby also means that your lover's
moods shift rapidly from enthusiasm to boredom and back

again. He seems to be in a state of perpetual motion. The honey bee flitting from flower to flower. Just when you think you have him pinned down, he's off nibbling at another variety. It's maddening and fascinating. It's also the charm in the Gemini mystique, and once bitten, it's fatal!

And so you've fallen for the Peter Pan of the zodiac. A lover blessed with youthful charm (he'll look 30 when he's 50) and one who finds it quite easy to charm the pants off most women, figuratively and literally.

Did I mention that Gemini knows a little about a lot of things? Actually, some critics accuse him of being shallow because his knowledge never goes very deep. That's simply because everything appeals to him; there just isn't enough time in his lifetime to delve into it all. But people who underestimate Gemini usually live to regret it -- because the spark of his genius can ignite at any time.

WHAT TURNS HIM ON?

In case you were never really sure, a woman with a brain is a *very* sexy creature to Gemini. If she's lucky enough to combine brains with good looks and charm, the result is devastating. There's no better example of this than Jacqueline Kennedy who had the brains, beauty and mystique to capture her famous Gemini husband, John F. Kennedy.

Nothing makes Gemini feel sexier than a woman with enough brain power to keep up with his intellectual gymnastics. His mind is the fascinating product of the planet which rules it -- completely mercurial. He's the original mind-game champion and trying to stay one step ahead of him is not for amateurs.

The woman who seduces Gemini heart, mind, body and soul must first turn on his mind and his body will follow. Know a little about a lot of things (that's a Gemini talent). Read more than Ann Landers and start mixing a little PBS with your weekly diet of talk-really-is-cheap-shows.

Gemini will suffer through your weight losses, your latest emotional crisis, but if you bore him...gone!

Your lover is a collector of intriguing data. Expect clipped-out newspaper articles to arrive in the mail which he hopes will interest you. Want to interest him? Report that you just read about the discovery of a sexagenarian in the Himalayas who sustained an erection for 30 days while playing Old Man River on the kazoo. He'll fall madly in love with you.

He also likes you independent. Perhaps your lover has already been married (Gemini is like that old vaudeville act *Pete and Repeat*, he does everything twice), and if that's the case, he may be frightened by a helpless woman. Perhaps he needs to maintain the illusion that if he ever finds himself in a bad relationship again and wants his freedom back, the lover he leaves will be able to take care of herself. Whatever psychological reasons may be involved, he definitely finds your high-powered career a turn-on.

So a very good way of keeping Gemini is to let him know how well you did before him, and how well you intend to keep on doing, whether he's around or not, thank you very much.

But whether it's marriage you crave or simply to be with your fascinating lover under your own rules -- in order to seduce him heart, mind, soul and body (let us never forget our goal) you must show Gemini that you love keeping up with his quicksilver mind. Give him warm, stimulating companionship -- remembering that it's even more important than sex to a Gemini. Create a soothing environment in which his nervous system can relax, and it won't be long before your lover's fear of commitment is but a hazy memory.

WHAT TURNS HIM OFF?

Imagine a beautiful woman who suddenly swears like a Hell's Angel. A sophisticated stunner who finishes her dinner and then starts to pick her teeth! Those scenarios would be anathema to Gemini. He loves the chic, feminine and graceful.

Never make your lover feel that all you care about is that cottage with the white picket fence. Gemini has that awful chilled-to-the bone fear of commitment, remember? What you think are subtle hints about the joys of marriage, and the patter of little feet around the den, will resound like bomb blasts in his ears. If a marriage contract is what you want, then the idea must come from *his* mind, or so he thinks.

IS GEMINI A ONE WOMAN MAN?

The famous Hollywood legend and lover Errol Flynn typified the handsome, horny Gemini whose second career is seeing how many bikini panties he can add to his collection. However, contrary to what most people think, a faithful Gemini is not an oxymoron. You're just going to need a lot of patience and a very long leash.

I simply mean that your lover demands a sense of freedom. It's hard for Gemini to think about settling down with just one woman, even if he adores you. Will he be bored, he wonders? Will sex turn into a chore night after night with the same woman??? Poor baby, no wonder his nervous system so often resembles a jig saw puzzle.

It's up to you to quell his fears by showing him that you have as much curiosity about life as he does, plus limitless layers to your personality...and he's going to love the erotic layer about to be peeled!

However, If you're the type who lacks confidence and needs a man whose eyes never stray, then kiss your Gemini goodbye. It's that love of variety that keeps him in top shape, and mentally salivating at passing blondes, redheads and brunettes. Of course, the same curiosity that killed the cat, can do this cat in, too. After all, a woman can only watch her lover ogling other bodies for so long before she picks herself up, dusts off her ego and leaves.

But don't panic, once this man is sure of your love, he can relax and begin to love you. That's the way it works with Gemini. The more in love with you he becomes, the less he'll look. He may never give up this time-honored sport entirely, but soon he'll just watch those gorgeous bodies for the aesthetics. After all, you'll be giving him the incredible erotic moments he needs at home, won't you?

DO YOU HAVE WHAT IT TAKES TO SEDUCE GEMINI?

Are you ready for Mr. Right when he finally comes along? Or were you so much in love with the concept of finding the perfect prince that you forgot to think about what *he* might want?

Do you read books? Gemini does. Do you love to travel? Gemini is ready to pick up and go at the drop of his American

Express card. How many languages do you speak? That's right,
the man who has you crazy about him also has a natural talent
for learning languages. That's why his sign rules the mind, the
hands and the tongue.

The key word is *interesting*. It's what you need to be to get
this fascinating man.

Until you do get him to commit only to you, it's best not to
show jealousy when you catch Gemini harmlessly flirting. It
will only annoy him and make him feel closed in. Besides, flirting is second nature to this man. He can no more stop charming
women than stop admiring his own wit. Trust Olivia, it really is
relatively harmless. So if you have a healthy ego and can laugh
it off, you'll do just fine. All others please pick up your box of
Kleenex at the door.

WHAT COLOR TURNS HIM ON?

Yellow is Gemini's color. It's the color of optimism and faith
in the future, and that fits your lover to a T. He's always sure
there's a rainbow and pot of yellow gold waiting at the end of
the next thunderstorm.

That's why he'll love your yellow chiffon nightgown. The but-
ter-yellow scented candles on the nightstand by your bed. The
pale yellow roses in the china vase. And if you're wondering if
they make gold satin sheets...ask your lover, chances are he's
already had them monogrammed.

WHAT'S HIS WORST FAULT?

I'm afraid that fickleness is high on the list. Just as Gemini
can tire of a subject and switch gears in mid vowel, so can he
tire of the *lover du jour*. "Out of sight, out of mind" must have
been dedicated to this mercurial fellow.

Another dubious asset is Gemini's ability to talk his way out
of most anything. He has just the right words for the moment. If
you have any suspicions about his veracity, just smile sweetly
and wait until either time or your private investigator proves
you wrong.

DOES HE HAVE A BAD TEMPER?

Gemini is rarely crude in any way, and he would consider a
loud outburst of temper nothing more than tacky.

However, that doesn't mean his caustic tongue isn't capable of
drawing blood. Remember, he's very articulate and never loses
an argument for lack of just the right lethal barb. Ouch!

IS GEMINI GOOD WITH CHILDREN?

Unfortunately Gemini is only fond of children when they
grow old enough to become interesting. Remember, I told you
that even beautiful women with childlike minds will send him
running. Perhaps he wants to be the only irresistible child in
the spotlight. Or perhaps he shies away from the responsibility
children represent. After all, Gemini is really only comfortable
being responsible for himself -- that's why getting him to settle
down is only for the strong of heart.

WHAT DOES GEMINI CALL HOME?

He likes space, bookshelves for his voluminous reading material and a general light, airy feeling. Having picture windows is
a plus, so that he can keep an eye on what's going on around
him.

He loves gizmos and gadgets. Gemini is the man who has a
television in every room, including the miniature in the bathroom, and radios pop up everywhere you wouldn't expect.

If your Gemini doesn't as yet have a telephone in the bathroom so that he can call all his friends while taking care of business, it's only because he hasn't yet thought of it. However, if he
excuses himself to go to the men's room and disappears for an
hour or so...you can bet he's thought of it!

As for the kitchen, your lover may spend less time in it than
at his family reunions, but you can bet that it will have the latest shiny gadgets on display. The automatic potato masher, the
slicer that can decimate a five pound squash in a single stroke,
etc. Gemini is putty in the hands of a good door to door salesman. Maybe it's because he's the ultimate salesman himself and
appreciates a good pitch when he hears one.

WHAT'S THE MOST SENSITIVE PART OF HIS BODY?

Gemini rules the hands, arms and tongue. Ah, what a playground!

Since your man has a sensitive nervous system, and when under stress needs all the soothing you can muster, I suggest you treat him to a wonderful massage.

Oh yes, Gemini also rules the bronchial tubes, and smoking is very dangerous. Unfortunately, so many of this sign do smoke because they tend to be so highly strung. The end result is that your lover will get stressed out and his respiratory system will suffer for it. Some steady erotica has been known to ease Gemini's nerves in time.

Now for the massage.

Every artful massage must start with the right lighting. Kill those 100 watt bulbs and instead, light soothing, scented candles. Slowly take off your lover's shirt, tell him to lie back on soft pillows and unwind...while you put music on the stereo, something beautiful and peaceful like South American flute music, and then...

Using a wonderfully erotic massage oil, start with the hands. I told you that Gemini rules the hands, and you will be delighted to find out how very well he uses them. *Patience!*

Now begin by slowly, sensuously stroking each finger. Pull on them hard, all the way to the tips. The webbed part between the thumb and the index finger is particularly sensitive. It's a favorite spot of acupuncturists who will tell you that it leads straight to the stomach. After you've properly kneaded it, roll your thumb inside the palm of his hand. Then start working your way up his arm, all the way to the shoulder. The inside of his elbow. His sleek biceps. Make all your movements slow and seriously sensuous.

They say (those sages that who know everything) that the healthiest way to live is in the present, not ruminating about the past or worrying about the future. A wonderful shoulder massage will make your lover do what he rarely does -- actually unwind and totally immerse himself in the moment. As for that other part of the body that Gemini rules, the tongue, we'll just leave you to your lover, your privacy, and your imagination.

HOW DO YOU DRESS FOR A GEMINI?

This man has sophisticated tastes and his love of variety can
be fun to satisfy. Don't get stuck in any one "look" but surprise
him by being perfectly comfortable wherever he takes you. He'll
love you "down and dirty" hiking in jeans, or elegantly dressed
for the theater. He'll even love your imagination dressed in
"costume" now and then -- a gypsy look with bangles up your
arm...shimmering Indian scarves and gold earrings...
     Gemini has a liking for geometric patterns and prints, too.
The fellow in the checkered sports jacket is probably a Gemini --
and don't be surprised if your lover mixes patterns that would
raise the eyebrow of a Wall Street banker. If that conservative-
looking banker is a Gemini, chances are that underneath his
pearly gray suit is a pair of wild patterned Jockey shorts.

RECIPE FOR A PERFECT EVENING

Taurus may treat a gourmet dinner like a religious experience,
but Gemini is too restless to stay anywhere for long. That
includes sitting down to a relaxed meal. Because he also hates
to eat alone, more often than not, your lover is used to eating on
the run. He's the fellow who loves Chinese food because he can
eat straight from the cartons. Remember how sorry you felt for
the poor baby when you opened his refrigerator door and saw
all that white staring back at you?
     Gemini's cell salt is Potassium Chloride which strengthens
the fibrin in the blood. If you start caring for this man's physical
needs, then remember what foods are important for him: asparagus, apricots, oranges, peaches, pears, plums, beets, celery and
pineapples.
     Herbs used in your cooking are of vital importance. For
Gemini, parsley helps to relieve his eye strain and purify his
blood. Also, skullcap (try it as a tea) is good for all kinds of nervous ailments due to stress. If it sometimes seems like your
lover walks a fine line between healthy tension and a complete
nervous breakdown, give him a nightly cup of this tea and a
good massage.

     Note: This suggestion is relevant for all the signs. It's impor-
tant to cook with love (I'm convinced it makes all food taste better), but do even more for your lover and buy foods at natural

food markets. When it comes to taste, organic vegetables and fruits are in a class by themselves -- and just knowing you're putting chemical-free foods in your body makes you feel all the more spiritual and healthy.

The only temptations able to lure Gemini to enjoy a full meal are good companionship and witty conversation. I can provide the recipe to intrigue Gemini's palate, but the wit, my dear, is up to you.

FIRST STEP:

Although your lover is used to "eating on the run" -- that doesn't mean he can't appreciate a beautiful table setting and fine food. If you're nervous and want some conversational support, it will be perfectly okay to invite your most interesting friends to join you. However, *interesting* is the key word here. Gemini loves provocative conversation, but endless small talk and nice but boring guests (and it doesn't matter if she is your dearest friend since the 8th grade!) will have Gemini looking at his watch and then for an escape.

Note: Olivia suggests that beautiful women *not* be among the invited guests. After all, our flirting Gemini doesn't need another woman whetting his sexual appetite, now does he?

So, put out that pale blue tablecloth or place mats, set the yellow candlesticks just right, and plan what will be one of your most delicious memories.

SECOND STEP: LUSTY GREEK SALAD

You may serve the salad with the meal or before. By the way, I've made the ingredients feed six people, just in case you decide to invite guests.

2 medium heads of iceberg lettuce
1 minced clove garlic
1/4 tsp pepper
1/4 tsp thyme
1/4 tsp rosemary
1/2 cup olive oil
3 tbs tarragon vinegar
1 tsp salt
2 cups white bread diced

2 tsb Worcestershire sauce
2 tsp chopped tarragon
1/3 cup corn oil
3/4 cup Feta cheese
10 black olives

Wash the lettuce thoroughly and then store it in the refrigerator so it will be nice and crisp. Then put garlic in olive oil and let it stand a couple of hours. Throw away the garlic and strain the oil. Combine the vinegar and Worcestershire, slowly add the olive oil and beat for 5 minutes. Add the tarragon, salt, pepper and herbs. Sauté the bread in vegetable oil until it's golden brown, then drain thoroughly on paper. Place the lettuce in salad bowl and add cheese and olives; pour the dressing and toss. Sprinkle with croutons.

You may want to serve garlic bread with this, and you'll find the recipe for it under Aries.

Don't forget one of the most important ingredients of the evening -- a good wine. Since the food is Greek, you can serve a Greek wine or a Rosé or burgundy will also be fine.

THIRD STEP: EGGPLANT EROTICA

4 tbs chopped onion
2 tbs butter
2 cans (6 oz) tomato paste
1 tsp oregano
1 tsp basil
1 tsp parsley/salt
1/4 tsp pepper
2 medium eggplants peeled and sliced
2 well-beaten egg
1/2 cup milk
1/2 cup bread crumbs
4 tbs sesame seeds
2 tbs olive oil
2 cups grated Kefalotyi cheese

Sauté the onion in butter and add tomato paste, oregano, salt and pepper. Simmer for 10 minutes. Remove from heat.

Dip eggplant slices in the mixture of egg, milk and salt; then in a mixture of bread crumbs and sesame seeds. Fry in olive oil in skillet until it's golden brown, turning over once. Heat the oven to 350 F. Arrange alternate layers of eggplant, cheese, tomato sauce in large (or two smaller) baking dishes. Plan to end up with the cheese on top. Bake about 30 minutes.

INTERMISSION:

Assess the dinner conversation: if your lover has a glazed look and you don't know if that's a smile on his face or if he just dislocated his hip, then get an immediate headache and tell your friends that, gosh, you're soooo sorry, but this migraine is terrible and would they mind skipping dessert and say goodnight early?

However, if the talk is flowing and your Gemini is a happy camper, then leave them to their fun and slip into the kitchen to put the light under the coffee maker.

FOURTH STEP:

You can stop by a Greek pastry shop and pick up some prepared dessert. Or, if you're *really* in love...

NUT N' HONEY

1/2 cup honey
2 cups sugar
1/4 cup water
2 stiffly beaten egg whites
1/8 tsp salt
1/4 cup chopped almonds
1/4 cup chopped hazelnuts
1/4 chopped walnuts

Combine the honey, sugar and water in a saucepan and cook until it all reaches thickens. Combine egg whites and salt; add the syrup gradually, beating constantly until the mixture stands up in peaks. Spread into a shallow 10-inch pan, well greased, of course. Top with the nuts.

After it cools, cut in rectangular pieces. It will make about 24 delicious pieces.

WHERE IS THAT ROMANTIC GETAWAY?

Nothing is sexier than to be with this particular lover in an exciting, cosmopolitan city. Gemini really knows how to appreciate the fast pace and endless variety.

This sign rules London and that's always a wonderful destination in anybody's fantasy. However, if this is the week your budget won't even allow for bobby pins, much less for bobbies in Picadilly Circus, then your lover will still be like a little boy in that candy store called New York.

Gemini will be able to hop from art galleries on the east side to trendy restaurants in Soho -- never staying anywhere long enough to yawn. After a wonderful night of theater, then drinks in some legendary jazz spot (there's at least one on every block in the Village), you'll find your way back to the privacy of that beautiful hotel overlooking Central Park.

The champagne will be chilled...while you and your man will soon be anything but! Nestled in his arms, he'll talk about jogging in the park tomorrow...he would even like to get a very early start...and as you undress, you smile and murmur that he'll probably be much too tired for jogging...is that a promise, he smiles back...trust me, darling, you say, you're going to be so wonderfully exhausted, so blissfully spent that you won't be able to move a muscle...and as a matter of fact, you add, slipping in between the cool sheets, you'll be *so* tired that you'll probably ask me to lift it for you...he laughs, that's what I call dead, not tired, he says...and you both giggle like naughty kids...and as he turns out the light he whispers huskily...well, on second thought...perhaps a hansom ride around Central Park is a better idea...

HOW TO PLEASE A GEMINI SEXUALLY.

Most relationships start on the telephone. Remember those summer nights as a teenager alone in your room, lying on your bed in your panties,with the lights out, the cool breeze blowing softly through the lace curtains and your boyfriend on the other end of the phone line? Somehow the subject of algebra never got spoken.

Do you remember that exquisite feeling of touching yourself while listening to the sound of his breathing during those long pauses when neither one of you wanted to hang up, but neither could think of anything to say? That's when, "What are you wearing?" and…"Where is your hand now?" came into creation.

Well, now you're older, but that only means that you're wiser and you *know* just how good phone sex can be.

Reach out and touch someone…

What you're about to do stimulates the mind which is the sexiest organ in the body. Never forget a sage bit of advice from Olivia…mental stimulus is very important to your lover. Always think about how to make *him* think. It's the key to his mind, his heart, his libido, and probably his safety deposit box!

As I told you, once you capture his fascinating mind, his body will soon follow. Besides, being surprised sexually is a great Gemini turn-on, and receiving the following phone call from you will definitely give him one unforgettable surprise party.

Speak low when you speak love.

You're going to let your voice be the erotic instrument it was meant to be. Begin by speaking very close to the mouthpiece. Pretend that your other jealous lover is asleep next to you and you don't want to wake him. It doesn't matter if your Gemini is calling from Nome, Alaska, as far as you're concerned your mouth is two inches from his lips.

Naturally, it's important that you set your own stage for this performance. Is the red light bulb in place of the daytime white? Or candles? Is your favorite music on the stereo? Perfect. When you're totally naked, lie down on your bed and telephone your lover.

Listen to the heat…

Sooner or later (and in this case, the minute he hears the purr of your voice it will be sooner) he'll ask: what are you wearing?

Now in exact detail, Olivia wants you to describe the following movements to him…precisely as you are doing them.

You are wearing nothing but a beautiful, long, pale, yellow silk scarf around your neck. Tell him to picture this in his mind; then say that you want him to completely undress, too.

While he listens to your warm, loving voice, slowly orchestrate the removal of his clothes -- telling him each piece of clothing to take off. No, you instruct him, don't take that sweater off so quickly. Lift it slowly, slowly over your head. Lower your pants the same way, feeling them slide over your

ankles. Now, ask him to tell you when he's completely naked.
Order him to lie back and feel the bed beneath him...how heavy
his calves, buttocks and shoulders feel against the bed. Tell him
to close his eyes and sink deep into the pillow.

It's important that he shut out the rest of the day-level world.
So instruct him to hear nothing but the sound of your voice and
to forget all those other people he is. To plunge deep down into
the peaceful darkness. If you didn't know it, the infamous
Marquis de Sade was one of the most erotic of Geminis -- so
never underestimate the power of your lover's imagination.

What you have done is to prepare him mentally for what you
are about to do to him physically.

Now as you turn on your side, tell him that the ends of the
silk scarf are slipping down between your breasts.

"They are like two strong, silky arms," you whisper, "your
arms. Imagine that I'm slowly reaching around in back of me
and pulling those silky arms between my legs...imagine that
your strong hand is gently turning me over on my stomach...
pulling the scarf tight until it enters me."

Let your own hand do what your lover would die to be doing
at this very moment. He will listen to your gasp and enjoy one
of the most enormous erections he's ever had.

Of course, a lady with manners will continue talking to her
lover until he's satisfied himself...and there's nothing left on the
other end of the line but a low, gratified growl.

Share the fantasy. . .

Another strong Gemini fantasy is to have sex while traveling.
This could be on any public transportation, hot air balloons
included, with just a seagull or two applauding from the balcony.

Or how about a simple little erotic interlude on an interstate
highway? Every girl should experience exceeding the sexual
speed limit like this. Naturally, you'll choose a time when the
traffic is minimal and if you're really a good citizen, you won't
even remove your seat belt.

So somewhere, on a cold winter night, when the windows are
all steamed and you're snuggled next to him, with the heat on
high, let your left hand stroke the inside of his thigh for a
moment. A long moment. Then lean over and put a tape in the
deck, unbutton your jeans and pull them down to your knees.

Then open the window enough to feel a cold breeze over your
legs and ask Gemini if he *really* needs both hands to drive.

CANCER

JUNE 22 – JULY 21

RULING PLANET: MOON

FEMININE, NEGATIVE, WATER SIGN

EROTIC DRIVE: TO FEEL

COLOR: SILVER

PASSION FLOWER: ANEMONE

MAGICAL SCENT: MYRRH

GEM: PEARL/MOONSTONE

METAL: SILVER

HERBS:

Butterbur   Violet   Ivy

"The average man is more interested in a woman who is interested in him than he is in a woman with beautiful legs."

Marlene Dietrich

Every woman has a bit of the actress in her, and now that you're in like, love or lust with a Cancer, you'll have a chance to play three starring roles: friend, lover and mother.

Cancer, ruled by the powerful moon, has the Crab as its symbol. I don't want you to think that means your lover will be "crabby" with his money, time or any other asset. Moon children are one of the most generous signs. It means, that like the crab, your lover will withdraw inside his shell if you step on his feelings.

Not only does the same moon that rules the fluctuating tides of the ocean pull on your lover's emotions -- but his is also a water sign. That means he is doubly emotional. Don't even try to act happy if you're not. You could be Natasha Richardson giving the performance of her life and your Cancer lover would sense the truth. He is a psychic sponge soaking up the emotions around him. However, it's not all weepy - being so impressionable also means that your Moon child will be receptive to that *new* fascinating creature in his life...your true erotic self.

Whether you realize it or not, you have fallen in love with one of the most romantic and faithful of men. He may not have the boyish good looks of that famous Cancer Tom Cruise, or the animal magnetism of another like Sly Stallone, but you may be sure that your man will turn the world you share into a cocoon; one that he will love, nurture and protect.

The Duke of Windsor, a role model of an idealistic Cancer, became the symbol of romance when he sacrificed everything for "the woman he loved." That's how your lover will make you feel -- like a beautiful, adored queen -- the only treasure in the world that he wants to possess. Now that's not too difficult for a girl to take, is it?

WHAT TURNS HIM ON?

At some time in his childhood a very significant psychological moment happened. The Moon baby took one look at his mother and decided that she was the epitome of the perfect female -- and that every other woman he ever met in his life would have to measure up to her.

Now I'm not saying that Cancer is even aware that he Freudian slipped way back then, but you will discover that your man has a strong attachment to Mom. So when the moment comes when he proudly tells you how much you remind him of *her*, consider it a major step in the right direction.

Also, remember this famous advice (that Olivia reverently follows) and repeat it to yourself three times daily: The beautiful woman tempts a man, the intelligent woman fascinates him, the good woman impresses him, but the sympathetic woman gets him!

The female who penned those words must have been inspired by an affair with a Cancer male.

WHAT TURNS HIM OFF?

An unaffectionate woman, no matter how passionate, will make Cancer very unhappy. Make that *miserable.* Your lover wears his heart on his sleeve and he requires a lot of hugging, kissing and reassurance to get him through the day.

Also, if you're moodier than he is, that's a bit of a problem. You see, Cancer's feelings go right to his stomach -- and his sign rules that area of the body, along with the digestive tract. Emotions really do affect his health. So, when he knows that you're angry with him, being the "psychic sponge" he is, he becomes immediately upset. If he can't cajole you out of your mood, then he gets very unhappy. He feels sick. You feel guilty. Mon dieu! Suddenly, you realize that loving Cancer means you have to try harder to control your own mood swings, too.

Well, they say that love is a growing experience, but does that mean you have to completely change? Totally sacrifice those delicious moments of sublime depression? Give up that satisfying sulking? No, don't worry, being his understanding self, Cancer will give mood-swing dispensation for PMS.

IS CANCER A ONE-WOMAN MAN?

By now you probably can guess that answer.

If you're fortunate enough to be loved by this man you can expect all-out loyalty (the kind you thought went out with the bustle). Not only will Cancer *not* fool around or stay out late carousing with the boys, but he'll remember your birthday and prop a pillow behind your head while he whips up coq au vin in the kitchen. Then he'll make mad, passionate love to you, bring you warm towels and a cold drink afterwards, leave you only long enough to clean up the kitchen and then be ready to love you all over again.

Really!

DO YOU HAVE WHAT IT TAKES TO SEDUCE CANCER?

Do you possess that unique merging of the nurturing earth mother and the erotic female? That's what it will take to seduce Cancer's heart, mind, body and soul. Yes, it is quite a provocative and rare combination, but Cancer dreams of nothing less for his erotic love life.

Like a nurturing mother, you must have the patience to really understand the complex nature of this man. Don't let his moodiness scare you away. Just like the phases of the moon, it will pass. And sometimes when your lover retreats into himself, it's for recharging his creativity. After all, it's in the silence of our own thoughts that great ideas are born.

WHAT COLOR TURNS HIM ON?

The smoky gray-greens of the sea will soothe Cancer. He also responds to the peaceful, serene vibrations of blue. Colors that speak of harmony and contentment are soothing to the soul.

Of course, white and silver are winning colors for this sign, too, and be sure to compliment whatever you wear with silver, the Moon child's own metal.

WHAT'S HIS WORST FAULT?

Olivia hates to divulge this bad press, but just as Cancer is ultra sensitive when it comes to his own feelings, he can be just as insensitive to the feelings of others.

For instance, he loves to entertain and will be crushed if the guests are not ecstatic over his bouillabaisse. He planned. He fussed. He slaved over it all day! He is the one who loves the dish, and if he had given it more thought he would have remembered how many others didn't. See what I mean?

DOES CANCER HAVE A TEMPER?

He does, but your lover sublimates his anger, and the result is that angry stomach. Learning how to communicate his feelings is one of the most important lessons you can teach him. The best way is always by example. For instance...

An emotion that ignites Cancer's temper is jealousy. Oh yes, your man tends to be possessive, holding you too close, convinced that you will somehow live up to his deepest ideals. (This may be the last man on earth who seriously believes in miracles!)

If you know that you've wounded Cancer by inadvertently making him jealous (Olivia will give you the benefit of the doubt here), talk to him about it. If you were playing mind games and purposely wanted to make him see green, admit to momentary insanity, bad genes, and swear on your grandmother that you'll *never* do it again. Do it before he pulls that shell down off his back and crawls inside.

IS CANCER GOOD WITH CHILDREN?

The same unconditional love the Moon Child brings to your relationship will bless his children, too. They complete his idealized picture of a perfect life: home, loving wife and children. This man is so good-natured, that picture could contain your Mom, Dad and mad Aunt Hester as live-ins, and Cancer would still be happy.

He may want to run off to many adventures in his lifetime, but he will always want to return home.

If he has a fault as a parent, it's not being able to let go. He'll be the doting daddy ready to give advice at any age, and that eventual thirty year old will always be his baby.

WHAT DOES CANCER CALL HOME?

It's a rare Cancer male who doesn't want to spend a lot of time in his home. Here is his retreat from the world.

Chances are that you'll find your lover's nest filled with things he's collected over the years. Don't immediately start planning which memorabilia you'll store in cartons once you move in, because every piece means something important to him. Each has a special significance, a cherished memory. Besides, it would be easier to persuade Imelda to give her shoes to the Salvation Army, than to get Cancer to throw his high school football away. He tends to be a bit of a pack rat and comfortable clutter is just fine with him.

As for how it's decorated, it can be modern, traditional or bohemian with many pillows on the floor and Japanese Shoji screens. It doesn't matter, because whatever the decor, Cancer's own warm personality will make it the true essence of a home.

HOW DO YOU DRESS FOR CANCER?

Think in terms of flowing garments that reveal the curve of your body. That means your treasured Armani suit with the macho shoulder pads will have to remain in the closet. This lover doesn't appreciate masochistic European designs either. You know, the ones that look as if they come with matching whips? Oh, well, maybe on somebody else's dominatrix!

Cancer prefers his lover totally and erotically female. A pastel cashmere sweater or blouse with a soft feminine neckline -- one that reveals the silver around your neck. A clinging long skirt, with a provocative slit up the side, oh yes.

RECIPE FOR A PERFECT EVENING.

Unlike Taurus, food comes second to Cancer.
What's most important in your home is the warmth it exudes. If your place gives off the right vibrations, you could serve Cancer yesterday's franks and beans and he'd be content. Of

course, he'll be happier if you do fuss for him -- because he really loves all the elements that make up a good dinner. He'll notice the colors on the table, the tapering candles, the pretty flush on your cheeks as you serve the bouillabaisse (you did learn how to make the damn thing, didn't you?)

Very important point: your lover is gregarious and a social animal. He loves get-togethers and people. One of his talents is being able to put strangers totally at ease, probably because he's so natural and unpretentious himself. But only invite friends to dinner who you know will be giving off -- as we say at Grateful Dead shows -- good vibes. The last thing you need is your man soaking up your girlfriend's terminal depression and ruining his digestive system.

Of course, many Cancer men get heavy in life because their bodies retain so much water. Plus your lover isn't one to exercise too much (out of bed, anyway.) Therefore, keep calories in mind when cooking for Cancer. Happily, he loves to eat fish and that's never too fattening if you go easy on the sauces.

The cell salt for Cancer is Fluoride of Lime. Putting enough of this in his diet helps everything from strengthening his teeth to keeping his back strong and his mental state well balanced. So you see, it's important to feed your Moon Child the right foods. Here are some of them:

Milk, cabbage, eggs, watercress, lettuce and pumpkin. The yolks of eggs are especially beneficial, as is whole wheat bread. Be sure to have dill and fennel on hand, too. These herbs, along with parsley, are especially good for our Moon child.

Oh yes, be sure to pick up some herbs that will help calm Cancer's nervous stomach. Water Lily is one, honeysuckle another. Just ask your local herbologist (that's the serene looking person in the white coat who seems to be blissfully zenned out) how best to use these herbs and if they're available as teas. Even plain old lettuce is a plant known to soothe Cancers.

FIRST STEP:

When you invite Cancer for dinner the first time, make it extra special by *looking* as if it's extra special. Surprisingly, this does mean something slinky and sexy. Your lover will be happy seeing you wearing just about anything with a special touch. That touch should be a pretty, frilly apron over whatever you have on.

Please don't panic and report me to NOW. Feminism is still

alive and well, it's just that an old-fashioned apron is the perfect symbol to offer a man who loves his home as much as Cancer. No, it *does not* say "I am your servant and slave in the kitchen." It says "I am woman: warm, maternal, nurturing and loving." In short, it says all the wonderful things about you that your own mother would tell him if she could only find out his telephone number.

Keep the apron on until you serve dinner and then, having sneakily tied a vicious knot beforehand, enlist his help in getting it off. Of course, nobody says that you can't be homey and kinky at the same time -- so, if he really loves the little frilly thing, well...keep that apron on...and nothing else.

SECOND STEP:

Now get little cocktail forks for the following hors d'oeuvres, or if your man is the kind who likes to scoop out the oyster from the shell with his upper teeth, that's all right, too.

OYSTER ORGY

2 dozen oysters
2 lemons
2 tbs horseradish sauce
8 tbs ketchup
Pepper grinder
Dark rye bred

For these oysters on the half shell, pry open the shell with a knife (Julia Child recommends a plain beer can opener) and wash out any sand and grit from the bottom of the bay. Drain and serve on a platter with decorative touches of parsley. Mix horseradish and ketchup. Have a pepper grinder on the table. Of course, it's important to note that you must *always* buy shell fish in a trusted, immaculate fish market.

THIRD STEP:

Ask him if he'd like a beer in a pony glass (called a "shooter" on the wharves of Annapolis) so he can eat the oyster and then wash it down with a shot of beer. If not, bring out the Chablis. Oh yes, most important is to always have glasses filled with cold spring water on the table. Cancer is a water sign and your man needs a lot of it to keep refueled.

FOURTH STEP: LUSTY LOBSTER

You can invite your lover over for an *Annie Hall* evening of lets-boil-the-lobster-together insanity, but since life never seems to go as smoothly or as funny as it does in the movies, perhaps you should prepare everything without him, here's what you need.

2 (1 1/2 pounds each) live lobsters
3/4 cup butter
1 cup chopped mushrooms
1/4 tsp pepper
1/2 cup soft bread crumbs
1 tbs Worcestershire sauce
dash Tabasco
1/4 tsp paprika
1/2 cup Parmesan cheese
2 egg yolks
1 cup heavy cream
1/4 cup brandy
3/4 cup sherry
4 tsp minced parsley
2 tsp salt

Cook and clean the lobsters and then take off the claws (they come off easily by twisting) and keep the smaller legs for garnish.

Crack the large claws and remove the meat, then dice it. Put the shells aside. Heat the oven to 350 F. Heat half a cup of butter in a skillet and sauté the mushrooms for a couple of minutes until they are lightly browned. Season with 1/2 tsp salt and 1/8 teaspoon pepper. Now add the lobster meat, bread crumbs, spices, sherry, brandy, cream and egg yolks. Season with remaining salt and pepper. Mix everything well and fill the lobster shells.

Grease a shallow baking dish and sprinkle the shells with cheese. Dot with the remaining butter. Just before you put it in the oven, sprinkle with paprika. Bake for 20 minutes. Put the lobsters on individual serving plates, decorate with the reserved small claws and serve right away.

FIFTH STEP: SUCCULENT SALAD

1/2 head Romaine lettuce
1/2 head Iceberg lettuce
1 red pepper cut into strips
Flavored croutons
1/2 cup Romano cheese

A few minutes before the lobster is ready, take the salad out of the refrigerator and pour your favorite salad dressing over it. Mix well until all the leaves are coated. Sprinkle with Romano cheese and serve.

SIXTH STEP: POTATO PASSIONATA

2 baking potatoes
1 cup shredded Cheddar cheese
1/8 tsp Tabasco
Sour cream optional

Preheat the oven to 450 F. Then scrub the potatoes well and rub the skins with a little salad oil. Place on the baking rack and bake them for about an hour or until the skins are tender when you pierce them with a fork. Melt cheddar cheese and mix with Tabasco.

Remembering to use mitts so that you won't burn yourself, remove the potatoes from the oven and immediately cut an inch cross in the top of each. Then take a towel and carefully holding the potato, press from the bottom until the white insides partially appear through the cross. Pour the cheddar cheese mixture into the potatoes.

Now if your lover is in pretty good shape, it's perfectly alright to spoil the man by serving sour cream with his baked potato. However, if his middle resembles a third trimester pregnancy, then I suggest you skip it.

Again, depending on his waistline, you might want to serve hot crescent rolls. If you decide yes, then put them in the oven for the last 3 or 4 minutes with the lobster and potatoes.

INTERMISSION:

After this spectacular meal your Cancer lover just might beg to move in lock, stock and baggage.

It's time to take him into the living room or den for some dim lighting, closer body contact and then...

SEVENTH STEP : IMMORAL MOUSSE

Serve a dark chocolate mousse cake, picked up at your favorite French patisserie and perk your best ground coffee. If you can make Expresso, then don't hesitate to treat him to the perfect ending to this sublime meal. Add cinnamon to coffee and possibly a dollop of real whipped cream.

WHAT'S THE MOST SENSITIVE PART OF HIS BODY?

Women are not the only creatures to find their breasts a wild erogenous zone. Cancer rules the breasts and if you don't know him that well yet, just arouse him by running your fingers lightly over his chest, *outside* his shirt, of course. Later, fondling his nipples (wait for details, they're coming) will drive your lover wild.

WHERE IS THAT ROMANTIC GETAWAY?

Cancer rules the ocean and it is always drawing him with its soothing, sensual rhythms.

Naturally, Venice and Holland, both with their romantic canals, are ruled by Cancer. However, it doesn't matter whether you find yourself near domestic waters in Miami or in the international milieu of St. Tropez. Just be there together and make sure it's during a full moon. That celestial time is pure magic. With his compelling ruling planet overhead and the vast ocean before him, your lover will be in his most receptive state for erotica.

Lying at the edge of the water, on an isolated stretch of beach (that you took the trouble to discover beforehand, of course) you feel as though the two of you are framed in the moon's spotlight. Your lover's fingers touch the edge of your bathing suit,

and you feel it falling...then comes the delicious sensation of
tropical waters caressing your breasts...now his mouth comes
down and gently, urgently does the same...and all you can hear
is the sound of your heart beating...and the music of the waves
lapping against your skin as...

HOW TO PLEASE CANCER SEXUALLY.

The first time you kiss, make sure that your lips come just
close enough to create body chemistry -- that spark that is only
there with the right person. Whether this happens while you're
washing the dishes and he's drying, or while dancing in the living room in front of the fire, or while sprawled on your white
bearskin rug, it's definitely *before* you take him to the bedroom.

Mommy knows best. . .

The reason I say *you* take him into the bedroom is because
this is the time in your relationship when you're going to play
the first of those three roles I mentioned -- mother, lover and
friend. In your maternal role, you will now take your adorable
baby's hand and lead him into your bedroom. There are red
bulbs glowing in the lamps, the sheets are fresh and the pillows
are fluffed.

"I want you to close your eyes, relax..." you purr into his ear
as you lay him down on the bed.

If you have a music box, now is the time to lift its cover and
have him concentrate on the delicate sounds as you unbutton
his shirt.

"Just let the world slip away..."

You gently stoke his collar bone, then let your fingers lightly
move down his chest.

"Now you're totally relaxed...."

Take your time to let the tips of your fingers soothe him to the
edge of sleep. Then just to test how well you've done, lift his
hand and drop it gently. If it falls like an oak, you've succeeded.

"Yes, you're a very good boy," you kiss him lovingly on the
forehead.

Now your fingers slip inside his unbuttoned shirt and slowly,
ever so slowly, let that body chemistry spark zap the tip of your
fingers...as you touch his nipple. He shouldn't feel pressure,
only that erotic energy as the nipple rises to your fingertips.

"I don't want you to become too excited," you whisper, "I want you to behave yourself. If you get a hard on, I'll spank you. Little boys aren't supposed to have hard ons."

If your lover doesn't bolt from the bed immediately from fear that he's slipping into a land that he only remembers in a primal way, then he's ready to play.

You've put Cancer in the strata of the Alpha state where it's warm, comfortable and totally natal-erotic. Don't forget to keep the music box playing.

After you've slowly taken off his shirt, put your mouth where your fingers have done the walking. With the same he-can-barely-feel-it-chemical-spark, let your lips slowly rotate over his erect nipple.

"Take a deep breath and hold it until I tell you," you say, "then imagine forcing that breath out through your nipples."

When he does what you tell him you will see his chest muscles tighten like a rock. Those beautiful muscles are under the total control of your sensitive fingers. Now is the perfect time, the moment when he least expects it, to bring your lips down gently, warmly, firmly on the steel of his chest and to gently run your tongue around his nipple.

Hanky spanky...

Your hand reaches down and glides over his stomach to where you told him not to have a hard-on.

"Bad, bad boy," you whisper. "What did I tell you would happen if you did that?"

Before he can even think of an answer, your hand is on his belt loosening it, and he hears your voice ordering him to lift up while you pull his pants down. Your voice is stern now, not mean, not bitchy, only maternally firm and softly disciplining.

"Look how naughty you've been." Your hand gently caresses his beautiful hard-on. "Now I'm going to have to spank you."

Instruct him to roll over on his stomach and when he does, tell him to go immediately back to sleep.

The bottle of body oil is on the bed table and now you pour some into the palm of your hand. Lightly, like touching the fuzz on a peach, ever so gently rotate your hand over his rounded cheeks. As he drifts on the edge of blissful sleep, sharply slap your palm down on his baby bottom. Then do it again, and again, and again.

However, since you are such a loving mommy, let your right

hand spanks while your left reaches in between his legs and caresses his exploding naughtiness.

After that it's up to you, you might want to go on to breast feeding or bathing and powdering him, or baby might be so cute that you want to just eat him up. These are steps Doctor Spock never told us. One thing is sure, you've given your Cancer lover a night he will remember over and over again.

Many Cancers will prefer to act out the Oedipus fantasy. In that case, go ahead, girl, and Mommy him to death!

Share the fantasy...

Now I want to tell you about a secret sexual fantasy of many Cancer men. They want to be more like dominant Capricorns in bed. So this is where Mommy says goodbye and the role of lover takes over.

Another night when the moon is right, when its shining softly through the window on your tender shoulders, let him know through your body language that you are submissive; that he has full control to choreograph the night.

His fantasy is to dominate your body and mind. Full control.

Your candle burns at both ends...

You may or may not be ready for the anal and oral sex this fantasy includes, and if you're not, perhaps you should reexamine the relationship, because you'll never really know the man until you explore his deepest fantasy. So if you have any reservations about anal or oral togetherness, at least talk about it with your lover.

In fact talking about it quietly in bed...whispers...hands gently exploring...is one of the most erotic experiences you can enjoy.

LEO

JULY 22 – AUG 21

RULING PLANET: SUN

MASCULINE, POSITIVE, FIRE SIGN

EROTIC DRIVE: TO PERFORM

COLOR: YELLOW/GOLD

GEM: RUBY

PASSION FLOWER: GERANIUM

MAGIC SCENT: OLIBANUM

METAL: GOLD

HERBS:

Eyebright   Marsh Marigold   Mistletoe

"She was wooing him all over again, but wooing him to a deeper attachment than he had previously experienced, to an unconditional surrender."

Mary McCarthy
"The Company She Keeps."

A love affair with a Leo should be part of every woman's life, whether it lasts a few sublime hours, months or years.

This fire sign, ruled by the sun, is symbolized by the proud and regal lion. Don't forget the word *proud,* because it is very important; abuse it and like the lion, Leo will toss his mane, draw himself up to his full grandeur, and shoot you a majestic "fuck you" look before he stalks away. Then he'll go off by himself to lick his wounds in private, because he'd rather die than have you witness it.

However, if you stroke your lover's ego, you can bask in the sunny warmth of his Leo nature: generous, loving, entertaining, romantic and loyal. This man, with his irresistible charisma, is a dreamer of bigger-than-life dreams. What's more, because he's blessed with tremendous energy and creativity, he can actually make them come to life. In fact, just about everything is bigger than life with Leo -- big dreams, big adventures, big...oh well, there are some blessings I'll let you discover for yourself! After all, you are the type of woman who likes to make her own discoveries, aren't you? Leo is a magnet for women who are really unique.

Now it's time to find out if you are unique enough, and woman enough, to seduce your king of the jungle, heart, mind, body and soul.

WHAT TURNS LEO ON?

I told you that the operative word with Leo is *big*, and that certainly goes for his ego. It's a wonder the poor baby can even walk around supporting such a heavy load all the time. That means receiving your steady praise is, quite literally, soul food for this man.

Because Leo is romantic and generous (a combination you'll find very easy to live with), he'll be constantly showering you with gifts. It doesn't matter whether he's wealthy or not, spoiling you will be one of life's pleasure.

For instance, mention that you love roses and he won't simply send you a bouquet, he'll buy you the whole bloomin' flower shop! But, there is a catch -- he needs to be told how wonderful he is. The minute your man feels that you're not adoring enough, that somehow his foot has slipped an inch off the pedestal, he'll become insecure, and an insecure lion is a sad sight indeed. It's also dangerous, because you risk having him turn to another female for emotional and physical stroking.

Even jealousy will turn him on (he loves it, as long as you don't get too noisy about it). Yes, I'm talking about *your* jealousy. If you're ever foolish enough to make possessive Leo jealous, you'll know the terror that strikes the heart of a gazelle when cornered by a 200 pound green-eyed beast!

Of course, just between us, if you are the jealous type, don't be masochistic and fall in love with this man. You see, it isn't even Leo's fault, he just attracts women like flies. Hmmm, could it be that honey he dabs on his...?

Now, if your ego is pretty healthy, sit back and enjoy watching all those hungry females validate your good taste. Leo will probably flirt back (his will-power is jello in this area) but if he loves you, he'll simple bask in the flattery and remain faithful throughout it all.

WHAT TURNS HIM OFF?

Leo assumes his royal role as the actor in the family, and hates to share the spotlight (naturally Cecil B. DeMille, the Hollywood legend, was a Leo). Any overt theatrics from you will be a turn off. So forget temper tantrums, raging jealousy and throwing anything harder than kisses.

Because he loves subtlety in his woman, put away the

turquoise eye shadow and opt for just a hint of subtle gold (it's
his color), and never upstage him in front of friends. Worse yet,
take Olivia's advice and never, never make the mistake of laughing at him in front of others. It's dangerous enough when you
might laugh at prideful Leo in private, but when it's done in
public -- the results are lethal!

Also, Leo isn't interested in women who aren't going places
in their careers and ambitions. Whether that's to be the head of
Paramount Pictures or to join an ashram in Sedona, it doesn't
matter. Leo simply admires a doer. Yet a totally independent
woman leaves him cold. Never forget that he is The King (he
never will!) and he wants to feel that you look up to him and
depend on him. Yes, it is a wee bit chauvinistic, but on Leo anything looks good. Robert Redford is a charming Leo who sup-
ports that claim.

IS LEO A ONE WOMAN MAN?

This might be Leo's most attractive trait, because once he
gives his love, he becomes a pussycat, purring contentedly in
your arms.

He will always be a terrible flirt of course, adoration from the
weaker sex is just too delicious to resist. There are times when
his flirting will drive you wild with the fear of losing him, but
the quickest way to have that happen is to show him that you're
jealous. He just wants to play, to flex his manly muscles every
now and then, to see the appreciation of his assets reflected in a
woman's eyes. That makes him feel ten years younger and
invincible. But never forget that he loves you, only you, especially because you understand the harmlessness of it all.

DO YOU HAVE WHAT IT TAKES TO SEDUCE LEO?

Even more than glamour, which he adores, the subtle and the
mysterious in a woman intrigue Leo. Hillary Rodham Clinton
has an elusive quality that people find very attractive, and none
more so than her Leo husband.

It's precisely that *different* quality about you that draws him.
Then you must have the self-confidence to keep him. Be as
affectionate, warm and passionate as you can be. You must also
share Leo's wonder of life, because inside your lover is the child

who still marvels at every sunrise.

WHAT COLOR TURNS HIM ON?

The orange-gold of the sun excites Leo...wear everything from vivid red to pure deep gold and every hue in-between. Gold candles in your bedroom, or perhaps a red gold candle holder will produce just the theatrical touch he likes.

Naturally, if you become crazy about this man to actually spend your money on a very expensive gift, make it a watch, make it a ring, make it a bracelet, but make it gold. Nothing will make the lion roar louder with appreciation.

WHAT'S HIS WORST FAULT?

His vanity can well be called his Achilles heel, because unscrupulous people can get Leo to do practically anything by stroking that ego of his. At his worst, Leo may look deeply into his lover's eyes and whisper: "Darling, you're the most incredible, brilliant, beautiful woman in the world -- you must be to have gotten me!" Well, if he doesn't actually say it, chances are he's thinking it.

Another fault is Leo's tendency to show off. It's true that he usually has a lot to show off about, but the more evolved Leo will let others discover his assets for themselves. However, that *other* Leo -- the less secure, boastful one -- tends to announce every great thing he has, or does, or plans to do, with an ear-deafening fanfare.

DOES HE HAVE A TEMPER?

Yes, your lover has a royal temper. What most people don't realize is that when the lion roars (and can he ever!) it's still fairly safe to get within three feet of him. It's when Leo becomes very quiet, when you can almost hear the dangerous swish of his tail, that you're in trouble. That's when you know your lion is deeply wounded.

The deepest wounds come when his pride has been slighted. Remember what Olivia told you about daring to laugh at this lover in public?

When he roars and carries on, don't worry about it. Leo does not hold grudges and just as quickly as his temper flares, that's how quickly its fire can be extinguished with a kiss.

However, when he becomes quiet and you know that it's not life threatening -- just the proverbial "thorn in his paw" -- proceed carefully, approach the great beast with caution...and see if you can gently extract what's hurting him. Of course, it's all worth it. Remember in the fable how appreciative the lion was after his friend the mouse removed the thorn from his paw? That's the expansive kind of Leo appreciation you can look forward to, and more!

IS LEO GOOD WITH CHILDREN?

Children love Leo immediately because they sense the child in him. Perhaps because, like most performers, Leo has a need to be loved, and he excels at entertaining people. There's no better audience than children, and that's one of the reason kids always treat him like an equal.

Most important, your man will make a wonderful parent because he treats children like the honest-to-goodness little people they are; he respects their individuality, he never steps on their pride, and he shares their every joy in life.

WHAT DOES LEO CALL HOME?

Even if your lover has been single all his life, chances are he'll opt to live in many rooms. The lion loves being able to roam about in a spacious lair.

If he can afford it one day, your Leo will have a penthouse in the city, a home in the country, a villa on a Greek island, a castle in Scotland, etc. This man does not have simple tastes. Wherever he lives, he'll want as much space as his budget can buy. Remember, this is one of the signs in the zodiac who thinks on a grand scale, who believes that *everything* belonging to him (including you) is a reflection of his treasured self-image. So, naturally, where and how he lives is of the utmost importance.

He doesn't like small and fussy furniture. His taste, once again, runs to the large and comfortable. Big, plush sofas (the sectional sofa was no doubt designed by a Leo)...in which he can sink, and overstuffed pillows on which he can rest his lionine head. Fabric? Leo loves the lush feel of velvet. Silk pajamas. Cool linen shirts. All the luxuries of life. Naturally, if he can feature possessions like grand pianos and swimming pools, so much the bigger and better!

HOW DO YOU DRESS FOR LEO?

Even though I'm far more interested in showing you how to *undress* for Leo, here's a few tips:

I told you that he prefers subtlety in his woman, but that doesn't mean gray business suits and blouses with those boring little bows. He'll take one look at that kind of outfit and turn comatose. The aura of glamour in a woman is a tremendous turn on for Leo.

Sean Penn is a Leo who was attracted to a lady known for dressing, and undressing, in her own unique and glamorous style. Of course, being a Leo herself, Madonna instinctively knew what would turn him on.

Yes, he likes color and bold, contemporary fashions, with just enough glamour to make them exciting. This is the man who actually knows the difference between what's new in Italian fashion this year and what's as cold as yesterday's pizza.

When it comes to what to wear in the bedroom, you can really have fun turning on his imagination. Your lover will get a great kick out of going shopping with you, and he'll respond to the most romantic to the most outrageous. Victoria's Secret to Frederick's of Hollywood and everything inbetween. Flannel is not his style. Neither is polyester. Stick to those silks and satins and fabrics that feel delicious against your skin...under his fingers...

RECIPE FOR A PERFECT EVENING

Leo has rich tastes in everything he does -- from the Rolls he dreams of driving one day, if he doesn't already, to the famous rich sauces of French cuisine. Leo rules the heart (and he has one of the biggest, kindest of hearts), so it's wise to cut down on the cholesterol in his diet.

What you do in bed in the way of cardiovascular workouts will really benefit this lover. I mean that you shouldn't do all the work. Leave some of the aerobics for your man -- it's a neat way of getting ultimate erotic pleasure and a clean bill of health from the AMA.

Have a snack of walnuts handy, too. This food is actually very beneficial for your Leo lover's heart. If you'll notice, the two halves of the walnut itself resembles the diagram of the heart. In fact, walnuts in a salad can make a delicious difference.

Leo's cell salt is Phosphate of Magnesia. Its specialty is helping to restore muscular vigor and the albumen in the blood. It can be found in the following foods: Lettuce, almonds, grains, cucumber, onions, blueberries, asparagus, figs, barley, cabbage, coconut and whole wheat bread.

Herbs to keep on hand are dill, fennel, chamomile. A more exotic herb to pick up is Mistletoe (great for a nervous heart, which Leo rules),

FIRST STEP:

The surroundings should be as glamorous and sensuous as possible for this most dramatic of signs. The right lighting is essential and there's nothing like the golden hue of candlelight.

Leo loves wine with his meals, so splurge and treat both of you to something really impressive. Just save one cup for the following recipe and the rest is for dinner. On second thought, if you can afford it, go for a second bottle.

As for yourself, this is *not* the time to dress very casually. Make what you wear sexy and if you have a gold lame top, wear it over a gorgeous black velvet skirt. Or, go in the other direction, and put it over a pair of tight jeans. Both will be perfect for Leo. Remember this man likes to be catered to. He must feel unique. That's why everything you do should say "this meal is special, because you're special in my life."

SECOND STEP: TANTALIZING TEASES

CAVIAR
CRACKERS
CREAM CHEESE

Greet your lover with hors d'oeuvres. Something simple like cream cheese on crackers, topped with caviar, will give him a little preview of how fabulous this meal is going to be. It's also the time to open that ridiculously expensive bottle of wine you splurged on.

THIRD STEP: COQ A LA LEO

2 medium onions, chopped
1/2 pound sliced mushrooms
1 garlic clove minced
2 tbs margarine
1 tsp salt
1/3 tsp pepper
2 (2 1/2 pounds each) chickens, cut up
1/2 tsp paprika
1 tsp minced parsley
1 cup burgundy wine
1 tbs whole wheat flour

Sauté onions, garlic and mushrooms in butter in a heavy skillet for a few minutes, then add 1/2 teaspoon salt and 1/4 teaspoon pepper. Remove them from skillet.

Season the chicken with remaining salt and pepper, sprinkle with parsley and paprika. Then brown in butter on all sides. Add wine, onions and mushrooms. Simmer for about 45 minutes or until chicken is tender when pierced with a fork. Remove to a pretty serving platter.

Blend flour into the sauce and simmer for about 3 to 4 minutes and then pour over the chicken.

FOURTH STEP: WILD, WILD RICE CASSEROLE

2 cups wild rice
boiling salted water
1 pound sliced mushrooms
2 medium onions chopped
1/4 cup whole wheat flour
1/2 cup whipping cream
2 cups chicken broth
1/2 cup slivered almonds

1/8 tsp thyme
1/8 tsp basil
1/8 tsp marjoram
1 1/2 tsp salt
1/8 tsp pepper

Cook rice in salted boiling water according to directions and drain. Sauté the mushrooms and onions until golden brown. Add cream and flour and stir slowly until smooth. Add the chicken broth, continue to stir constantly until thickened. Season with herbs, salt and pepper. Add the rice and onion mixture, toss lightly until blended.

Turn into a 1 1/2-quart baking dish and put in the oven for about half an hour or until liquid is almost absorbed. Sprinkle with almonds and serve.

INTERMISSION:

Now is the time to take your new lover on a tour of your apartment (you did remember to leave that sexy nightgown draped casually over the foot of your bed, didn't you)?

FIFTH STEP: BARE BANANA

4 bananas
3 tbs butter
3 tbs granulated sugar
1 tsp cinnamon
6 tbs (3 ounces) Creme de Cacao or a cordial
6 tbs. Cognac

Peel the bananas and cut in half lengthwise. If small, leave them whole. Sauté the bananas in butter until golden brown. Then in the same pan cover them with sugar blended with cinnamon -- top off with Creme de Cacao and cognac. Now for the big moment: bring this dish to the table and light it. Your Leo loves flaming desserts. Wait till the flames subside and then... bon appetit!

WHAT'S THE MOST SENSITIVE PART OF HIS BODY?

Along with the heart, Leo rules the back and spine. No doubt the first American to discover the joys of petite Japanese women walking up and down the spine was a Leo. You don't have to go quite that far to please him, just treat your lover to a first-class back massage.

After you've turned down the lights and made sure the music is playing softly, have your Leo lie down on the bed. Tell him to let the world fade away. You've taken off his shirt, and so now you have only to pour the massage oil into your palms. Rub them together a few times so your hands will be healing and warm on his skin.

Using the heels of your palms, knead your way up his back, and then return to your starting point low on his spine, take your thumbs and run them hard all the way up to his neck. He'll love the sensation. Then using those thumbs, get rid of the knotted muscles along his shoulders. If those tension spots are hard and bulge, and he winces when you press, keep working on them until they disappear under your fingertips.

After about ten or fifteen minutes of this, when he's lulled into a blissful state, gently awaken him by using your mouth. Plant light kisses from the base of his spine up his back. Of course, when he responds with delighted shivers, apply more pressure to those kisses, until your lover rolls over and gives you a proper thank you.

WHERE IS THAT ROMANTIC GETAWAY?

You know by now that Leo likes opulence in his surroundings, so it doesn't matter if it's a hotel on the ocean or a villa in France. If you can afford it, make sure it's first class all the way: glamorous, elegant and romantic.

Some advice from Olivia: it's better to enjoy the ultimate sexy, fantasy surroundings for a few days than a place far less wonderful for a month.

Let's imagine the dreamlike vacation spot you've chosen is England, where royalty and theater have always reigned. Your theatrical Leo lover should feel right at home in this country shaped like a lion. Even if you don't have the vacation budget right now to buy those tickets to London, you might in the future, so let's fantasize what it will be like.

Imagine staying in an honest-to-goodness castle (haven't we all dreamed of doing that?) Now you and your lover are lying in a massive four-poster bed in a cavernous chamber, lit only by the glow from a 17th century stone fireplace. Somewhere there are taxis and subways and a rush hour, but not here, not in this most perfect of all worlds.

The maid has placed a bed warmer under the covers, but happily, you brought your own -- your Leo's skin gives off a penetrating heat that warms you to your very soul.

Now your lover takes you in his arms and you let your body melt into his. Just as you begin to move to his rhythms, you stop -- there on the wall is a portrait of an early Royal staring haughtily down at you...for just a moment you feel shy, inhibited...but then your warm, loving Leo moves his beautiful body again...slow...sensuously...and you close your eyes...you can feel the blood rising into your thighs...to hell with it, you think, this night you're about to make your own history...

HOW TO PLEASE LEO SEXUALLY.

One night in your apartment, while you're relaxing on the couch, and you've put another log on the fire or lit candles, you tell your lover that you feel a need to play with your balls.

Yes, you read that correctly.

Making the most of this very theatrical moment, you place a beautiful Chinese silk box on your lap and take out two shiny silver balls, each about the size of an egg.

Then you tell him the following story...

What you have purchased in a Chinese shop are the historic legendary Ben wah balls, used for centuries as erotica for Chinese concubines. Today we hear the sound of chimes inside the balls, but in ancient times, and still possible to find today, were two different metals. One metal was placed in one ball and the second metal in the other ball. Both were then inserted into the woman's vagina as she lay in a hammock and slowly swung back and forth. When the two balls touched, the special metals created an electrical charge, stimulating everything that needed to be stimulated. By using muscle contractions, the woman learned how to give herself the utmost pleasure from the silver balls.

Let your fingers do the talking...

Now that you have your lover's undivided attention, let him watch as you slowly rotate both balls in the palm of one hand.

Accentuating the finger movements, you try to keep the balls on the perimeter of your hand, including your fingertips, as you rotate the balls. What practice will eventually make perfect is that you will one day be able to control the movement of those balls and they will magically rotate around the outside of your hand without ever touching each other.

Now you whisper in your lover's ear that you're practicing getting complete control of your balls...so that he'll trust you enough to let you play with his.

Yes, you read that correctly, too...

Leo's are rarely speechless, but we can guarantee at this moment he'll be silently eating out of the palm of your hand. It's important to remember too that Leo loves two things: long-prolonged-sensual-drive-you-crazy foreplay and to be at the controls. You've already given foreplay with your mind, now, as you begin to undress him on the couch, it's time to turn the controls over to him.

Box number two...

The second velvet box that you hand your lover contains a silver egg that runs on two double AA batteries, the western man's equivalent to those Chinese metals of yore. It can be purchased in any shop selling erotica.

Chances are Leo will be familiar with this delightful toy. However, all he has to do is take a look at the size, the shape, the battery -- let his gaze fall on the curve of your inner thigh -- and he'll do what many adventurous lovers have done before him. He'll go to the kitchen cupboard and get a bottle of honey.

Note: It's totally permissible for you to have the honey already on the table in a covered and beautiful Chinese bowl.

Now you may want an appetizer before going straight to this exotic food...so indulge yourselves in as much foreplay as you can stand before dipping the silver egg in the bowl and watching it slowly sink into that golden, sweet honey.

Let Leo pull it slowly, slowly back out.

A taste of honey...

If your lover hasn't already removed your panties, make sure
he completely undresses you now, and you must return the
favor, so that nothing that can stand in the way of your ultimate
pleasure.

With your lover holding the controls of the egg, lie on your
stomach and put your head in his lap, while you slide one hand
underneath him; slowly caressing him, teaching him what you
learned with those balls on the table. With the other hand, glide
him gently towards your mouth.

Now tell him with a slight squeeze that you are both at the
controls. Slowly rise up on your knees and let him insert the
honey-dipped egg.

When the rhythms have built to a frenzy, slide across his
body, drawing your legs up along his sides, turning to face him,
until you can feel him enter you. Sitting on his lap, you now
feel the exquisite sensations of both your lover's sex and the
vibrating silver egg inside you. At this point our camera merci-
fully pans over to the fireplace, as the flames dance wildly, as
your favorite music builds...builds...builds...

Share the fantasy...

What you want is to not only please your lover sexually,
but to satisfy one of his dominant fantasies: to be sexually
served.

Now we'll tell you how to satisfy another Leo fantasy: *exhibi-
tionism.* Suggest to him that you would like to make love in
front of mirrors. Olivia promises that you won't have to repeat
the idea twice.

It's important to give your imagination full-play when it
comes to costumes. What I mean by costume isn't the usual
French maid with the apron, or the uniformed schoolgirl outfit,
but the most titillating creations imaginable -- outrageous g-
strings, teddies, net stockings and bikinis. If you have any exhibitionist leanings yourself, won't it be delicious to totally
indulge them by parading in front of your lover, whetting his
appetite, and finally satisfying it with a lick of honey?

Don't forget for a moment what a turn on it will be to have
Leo lie back and watch you caress yourself. Or even to dance for
him. It will.feel wonderful to have his eyes devouring every

inch of you, anticipating your eventual love making. Knowing as much about this lover as you do now, it won't be a surprise to learn that he'll want to entertain you in the same way. If you have a man who is proud of his body, he'll really get into showing it off -- dancing for you in a room lit only by candlelight -- moving sensuously to the music.

Note: If your lover is self-conscious about dancing in front of you, then be sure to reassure him. Tell him how much you like his body, and if he protests that he has to lose ten pounds, tell him how much he turns you on, love handles and all. Make the moment, light and fun, because that's part of erotica, too.

Before he begins, remember to oil his body so that the glow from the candles will catch every curve, every muscle. Don't bother oiling your own body...by the time the evening is over it will be completely oiled from head to toe.

VIRGO

AUG 22 – SEPT 22

RULING PLANET: MERCURY

FEMININE, NEGATIVE EARTH SIGN

EROTIC DRIVE: TO SUBMIT

COLOR: DEEP BLUES, DARK GRAYS AND BROWNS

PASSION FLOWER: GLADIOLA

MAGIC SCENT: PATCHOULI

GEM: SARDONYX

METAL: MERCURY

HERBS:

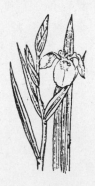      

Blue Flag   Marshmellow   Fennel

"If a woman hasn't got a tiny streak
of a harlot in her, she's a dry stick
as a rule."

D. H. Lawrence

When a Virgo male, the most discerning of all signs, discovers the rare jewel he decides to make his own, she has to really be treasure.

To carry this jewel metaphor a little further -- your Virgo lover will be proud of his prize and want to display it before the world. But he can't help constantly examining it for flaws, holding it up to the light and searching every facet of its inner beauty. Is it really perfect? Because perfection is what Virgo desires and sometimes he spends his entire life searching for it. Naturally, compared to this quest, finding the hidden needle in the haystack is child's play.

Prince Albert of Monaco may epitomize the picky Virgo who has all the "jewels" in the royal court for his choosing and still can't find the perfect one.

This earth sign, whose symbol is the virgin, is ruled by the planet Mercury. Like Gemini, your lover is governed by his head first and his heart second. But unlike Gemini who keeps his head in the clouds, Virgo's earthy nature makes him practical from his drip-dry shirts to his juice extractor.

Now don't go thinking your lover is as exciting as an allergy-free pillow, because underneath his buttoned-up exterior, Virgo has a highly erotic nature. He harbors wild fantasies of an earth mother type who will respect him, romance him and ravish him (in that order) and you may be woman enough to do it.

Most Virgo lovers are articulate, intelligent and creative. They are also known to be highly analytical and discriminating.

However, did you ever hear the theory that an asset in one setting can become a liability in another? That's exactly what happens with Virgo's critical ability. What makes him a keen ana-
lyst at work, can make him bloody unbearable at home. It's not
that he's mean, actually he *means* well, it's just that when it
comes to being highly critical, Olivia warns that the road to Hell
is often paved with good intentions.

On the positive side, your Virgo lover is interested in a long
and lasting relationship. Your brains matter to him just as much
as your beauty. Happily, romantic phrases don't glibly roll off
his tongue, so when they are finally spoken they always come
from the heart.

An interesting note is that Virgo is the rare sign that is actually very compatible with his own sign. Together they can criti-
cize the world and marvel at how incredibly perfect they are.

WHAT TURNS HIM ON?

For starters, a woman who is willing to work as hard as he
does, someone with a direction in life, a goal. Your lover is the
sign famous for putting in the necessary hours, and then overtime, to get what he wants. That fellow you see busily writing
in his day planner, scheduling every responsibility and goal is
probably a Virgo. But the planning he puts into his career goes
into his relationship as well.

Because he is such a dependable, hard worker, Virgo is often
taken for granted by the people who pay his salary. They just
expect the best from him and forget to compliment him along
the way. If your man has a healthy ego he may not be bothered
at all, but during those times when it hurts not be appreciated,
your Virgo needs to talk about it. Be sympathetic to his fears
about work, life, the future (whether they're real or just 3 a.m.
imaginings) and bolster his optimism.

Very often this sign suffers from an inferiority complex.
Remember the comedien who asked: "How good could a club be
that has me as a member?" That about sums it up.

It's no wonder Virgo always "comes up short" in his own
expectations since he expects perfection in himself as well as in
everyone else! Naturally, being only human he gets his ego
bruised again and again. So remember, kiss it where it hurts
and, most important, where it doesn't.

Next to making love to your beautiful body, Virgo will love

analyzing your mind, dissecting your personality layer by fascinating layer. (If he's not careful Virgo can analyze everything out
of existence, including love). He's an amateur psychologist and
gets turned on figuring out what makes you tick. Actually, a lot
of his psychological digging, whether he knows it or not, is
because he really does possess healing abilities. So don't be
afraid to share your interesting past, letting Virgo poke around
in it is a sure way to guarantee his role in your future.

Of course, it might be wise to leave out the time you ran off to
Tahiti with that married jazz drummer, who happened to be
your twin sister's transsexual boyfriend and...get the point?

WHAT TURNS HIM OFF?

There's one four-letter word that definitely turn your man off
and that is D-I-R-T! Yes, your Virgo lover adores cleanliness
and he'll notice it, or the lack of it, the minute he steps into
your home. There's an old maid quality about this man, which
can be really cute if it doesn't get out of hand.

If it does get a wee bit extreme, he can begin to remind you of
Felix in "The Odd Couple." This is one of the ways in which it
manifests itself. Virgo likes things clean, neat, in their place,
and the more lunatic fringe have been known to alphabetize
their spices.

When you're finally invited into his home, take a look in his
closet and you'll see that all the hangers face one way. The
darks are probably separated from the lights, and so on. My
God, you'll wonder, what does this man do with his Jockey
shorts?? (If you're lucky you may find out!)

Virgo just feels that life is easier to handle when it's neat. So,
if you've been living a little *casually* -- pantyhose fluttering over
a pile of Hilton monogrammed towels on the bathroom floor --
it's definitely time to clean up your act.

Oh yes, along with Gemini, your lucky lover belongs to a sign
that is able to keep their youthful looks -- and that means his
body probably looks as though it belongs to a man ten years
younger. Richard Gere is a Virgo who remains looking young
and incredibly sexy. So it makes sense that your man intends to
keep himself in excellent shape and will expect the same from
you. If you get lazy about exercise and your middle begins to
show it, you'll hear about it!

IS VIRGO A ONE WOMAN MAN?

Yes, even when a good-looking bachelor with deep pockets, Virgo will rarely be found in a lounge at *Happy Hour.* That kind of popular amusement is pure torture to this man who's basically shy and thinks small talk should be illegal. He's not the macho type, so posing at the bar with one hand on a beer and the other on any available thigh doesn't do a thing for him.

Plus, with Virgo's penchant for hypochondria, the thought of "picking something up" (and he doesn't mean a glove) from some body in a bar would send him running to the doctor for rabies shots!

So when your lover finally finds that jewel who fits his image of perfection, he's only too happy to give up the single scene. Unlike Aries who can be a tad chauvinistic, and mucho macho Scorpio, your lover really does believe in -- and will fight for -- women's rights. He'll burp the baby while you write your novel and will be the most stimulating intellectual companion and gentle lover you can find.

DO YOU HAVE WHAT IT TAKES TO SEDUCE VIRGO?

Like Gemini, Virgo finds an interesting woman sexier than a D cup. (Remember these two signs are both ruled by Mercury, so they have a lot in common.) You can turn him on by showing that you have a wider view of the world than reading Jackie Collins. Discuss politics with him, biographies, they're a favorite, classical music and poetry. All the serious mind candy on which your Virgo loves to feast.

This lover may not appear to be a sexual animal, but don't let those still waters fool you. Trust Olivia, there are raging currents underneath! Just because he doesn't come on strong doesn't mean he is not mentally making passionate love to you every moment. What makes his erotic nature even more intriguing is that it's hidden under defensive layers that will part like the Red Sea once touched.

So have the nerve to act on your desire...reach out...and touch!

WHAT COLOR TURNS HIM ON?

Stay away from those pink and blue pastels. Avoid bright lipstick colors, too. Instead, look to Mother Earth for some suggestions. Remember that Virgo is an earth sign and he loves the colors of a beautiful autumn day.

Bring those earth hues into your home and wardrobe. Russets, browns, golds, Virgo will love them all. And, of course, when it turns autumn, you can decorate your home with a lush bouquet of autumn leaves.

WHAT'S HIS WORST FAULT?

Picky, picky, picky. Olivia warned you that Virgo is a nit picker of the first order, and you've got to have a strong shell to withstand the barrage.

"You know I like my socks in *that* drawer"..."Did you leave the cap off the toothpaste *again*!?" So, at its worst, this can turn into nagging and all you can do is calmly straighten him out. Virgo is smart enough to hear it once, and intelligent enough to try his best to change.

In time your Virgo man will learn the most important lesson you can teach...to relate to you through his heart and not his head. However, be aware of something else: There are times when Virgo becomes so critical about the small stuff, to the point of really picking on you, that you can bet it's masking something bigger. Something is eating at his nerves that's apparently too sensitive to discuss.

Those are the times when you'll needs a lot of understanding, patience and love to find out what's really bothering him. You get a medal and a half if you manage to do this, since the urge to poison his protein shake will be overwhelming.

The irony here is that Virgo loves to dissect other people's emotions, but when it comes to understanding his own, and then actually revealing himself to a loved one, he finds it very difficult. The first time he tries baring his soul, poor Virgo will feel like that terrible nightmare in which we find ourselves perfectly naked in the midst of a crowd. But give him time, it will get easier as your love grows.

DOES HE HAVE A TEMPER?

Happily, your man is not the type to bang doors, throw vases
or ever, perish the thought, raise his hand. If anything, Virgo's
temper can manifest itself by being cruelly critical. But as I told
you, when that criticism gets out of hand, it just means that
something important -- something he's afraid to face -- is really
nagging below the surface.

So, whatever you do, don't return the sarcasm, but *calmly,*
point out to him that he is being hyper-critical. Could it be, you
lovingly ask (with all the patience of Mother Teresa) that something is bothering him? Something that he'd like to talk about??

He may not immediately dissolve into lovingness, but it won't
be long before you'll reap the rewards for that patience.

IS VIRGO GOOD WITH CHILDREN?

Your man is one of the most caring signs in the zodiac. His
only problem is that all too often, especially with his children,
he shows his caring in nagging and he forgets to add enough
warmth and affection.

His obsession with cleanliness can turn kids into instant neu-
rotics as they're told not only to pick up their clothes off the
floor, but to iron them, fold them and put them away. Well, I
might be exaggerating a wee bit here, but it's true that if the nest
isn't neat, Virgo daddy can turn into Mommy dearest!

So teach your lover how to relax and become a friend to his
children as well as a parent. That means getting down on all
fours in the yard to play with them, easing up on the rules, and
remembering that dirt washes away easier than tears.

WHAT DOES VIRGO CALL HOME?

Virgo has even more in common with Gemini when it comes
to liking gadgets. But where Gemini's gadgets may be found in
every room *but* the kitchen...your lover's kitchen will be lived
in and enjoyed. Spotless, of course. All those copper pots
shined to perfection.

He also likes to keep his restless eyes busy, so not only will
you find a lot of books on his shelves, but patterns such as
stripes on his walls and in materials, as opposed to flat colors.

But whether he lives in a spacious house or tiny apartment, you can bet your Hoover that Virgo's lair will be neat as a pin.

HOW DO YOU DRESS FOR VIRGO?

Save your naughty dress fantasies for the bedroom, because in real life, and especially in public, your Virgo lover wants you every inch a lady. To him a lady doesn't wear fishnet stockings, necklines that plunge to the knees and so on. He likes everything subtle, understated and very classy.

Of course, once Virgo lets his hair down (more on how to arrange that coming soon) you can play wonderful erotic games with him. There's a very earthy sensuality waiting and winking behind his careful exterior. What a turn on for this man to take you out to a very up-tight, proper business dinner -- to have you sitting next to him dressed like your daddy runs the church -- and know that you're not wearing a stitch of underwear. Oh yes, Virgo, as we will see, can be one of the kinkiest fellows around.

RECIPE FOR A PERFECT EVENING

What's that old saying...some people live to eat, others eat to live? Virgo is definitely in the latter category. He's not one to eat a lot of meat and usually sticks to just chicken and fish. He's probably well on the road to becoming a vegetarian.

To really impress him, serve a vegetarian/macrobiotic meal. Whether he's already into these natural foods or not, he will be absolutely thrilled that you're smart enough to investigate foods that are delicious and healthy too.

You may or may not be adventurous enough to serve your lover the following Japanese meal, but one thing is certain: keep those steaks in the freezer when you make dinner for your Virgo.

Virgo's cell salt is Potassium Sulphate. Enough of it will insure everything from a healthy liver to a dandruff-free scalp. So take note of what foods it's found in: lettuce, radish, tomato, carrot, rye, whole wheat, oats, endive.

More than any other sign, Virgo needs all the herbal help he can get to stay calm and centered. Fennel and dill are two important herbs to put in your cooking. When your lover is upset, you'll notice he often puts his hand on his solar plexus.

Skullcap, along with helping to soothe his nervous system, strengthens the solar plexus, the seat of fear.

FIRST STEP:

If you've never experimented with the delights of tofu and miso, both derivatives of soybean and high protein foods, you're in for a pleasant surprise. Lovers who eat macrobiotically (John and Yoko did) swear by it for health, youth and general nirvana.

Now, here is what you have to do to prepare for this meal. First and foremost, *clean everything that doesn't move.* Remember that your lover is fastidious and will notice any crimes of hair on the bathroom sink, face powder in the sink, dirt around the sink and...you get the idea.

Crisp tablecloth, sparkling glasses, the smell of wood polish and Lysol in the air -- mmmm, for a Virgo, that's better than Chanel.

Creating a bit of oriental atmosphere will add a touch of fun to the evening -- and it does go along with the menu. So take a trip to Chinatown and buy some pretty bowls for the soup and anything else that catches your eye. Bamboo placemats? Chopsticks are optional.

SECOND STEP: VIRGIN MISO SOUP

Visit the nearest health food market and pick up any of the foods listed here that you know are not found in the supermarket. Daikon is a Japanese radish and Wakame is seaweed. Before you say never, try it! To begin with, seaweed is really delicious in miso soup and it gives you more minerals and vitamins than you can count.

Let's put it this way, all the pretty lingerie and candlelight won't let you enjoy sex if you don't have the energy for it. So, eat healthy!

    1 pkg. Wakame sea vegetables
    1 quart spring water
    2 tbs Barley miso
    1 Daikon cut up
    1 cup thinly sliced onion
    1 vegetable bouillon cube
    Grated ginger

Rinse the wakame in cold water and let it soak about 3 minutes. Then cut it into half pieces. Place the wakame, bouillon cube, miso and onions in pot and add water. Bring to a boil, cover, and let it simmer 20 minutes. Since I'm not a purist (that bouillon cube takes the edge off the foreign taste), you are allowed to put in as much salt, pepper, garlic, parsley, etc. as you like. However, grated ginger is a favorite topping.

Note: Be sure to reduce heat while miso is cooking to save the beneficial enzymes.

COPULATING CASSEROLE

Again, any ingredients that look strange to you will be found in your health food market. Note: Be sure to wash vegetables especially well, removing any signs of Mother Earth from the leaves of the kale, etc.

1 cup diced tofu
4 cups cooked brown rice
2 cloves garlic, minced
1 medium carrot, sliced
2 large onions chopped
2 cups Kale chopped
1 1/2 cups broccoli flowerets
2 medium tomatoes, chopped
1/4 cup olive oil
1/2 cup Parmesan cheese
1-1/2 cups grated Cheddar cheese
1/4 cup bread crumbs
3 tbs tamari soy sauce
1 cup cashews
1/2 tsp salt
1/4 tsp black pepper

Partially steam the broccoli and carrots. Heat the oil in a wok or frying pan and sauté the tofu, garlic, carrots and tomatoes for 5 minutes. Add the kale, broccoli and sauté for 3 minutes longer. Combine the rice and vegetables in a large bowl, add salt and the remaining ingredients (hold back the grated cheese).

Transfer to a 2 quart casserole dish, cover and bake at 350 F for about 10 minutes, then remove the lid. Mound the grated cheese around the dish and sprinkle with cashews - bake 10 minutes more.

Note: Another nice touch will be a bottle of fine Chablis.

INTERMISSION:

Just sit and mellow out with the wine. When it's time for dessert, your lover has a liking for simple fresh foods such as...

FRESH FRUIT FANTASY

2 cups fresh or frozen strawberries
1 cup orange slices
1 cup pineapple chunks
1 cup watermelon chunks
1 1/2 cups seedless grapes
1 cup shredded coconut
1 cup orange juice
1/2 cup mineral water
1 to 2 tbs honey

Cut the fruit into bite-sized pieces and put into fancy goblets. Mix the orange juice with enough honey to get the desired sweetness and gently coat the fruit with the sauce. Sprinkle with shredded coconuts.

INTERMISSION:

FOURTH STEP: BANCHA TEA AND DESSERT

You can buy this tea in any natural food store, it's a different and surprisingly mellow taste.

WHAT'S THE MOST SENSITIVE PART OF HIS BODY?

Virgo rules the digestive system, bowels and intestines. That doesn't sound very erotic, does it? You'll just have to give this man a total body massage and make sure all his juices flow to their proper places. With Virgo, getting his juices to flow calmly is very important. This sign, more than any other, is under a lot of stress. What causes the stress?

Worry, of course. Virgo is the prime worrier of the zodiac. Being a perfectionist isn't easy and tends to turn people into nail biters. Most of what he worries about never comes to pass (he really does sweat the small stuff) but a massage will work wonders on his nervous system.

By now you know that a massage starts with the right lighting and just the right music, because atmosphere isn't just anything, it's *everything*. When the mood is set, undress your lover slowly and have him put his head in your lap. Begin to massage his scalp, pulling on the roots of his hair very gently.

Now pour a few drops of that musky massage oil into your palms and rub your hands together. The oil should be nice and warm to the touch. Treat your lover to how deliciously sensual it is to get a facial at an expensive salon. Using your thumbs, follow the curve of his cheek bones from the nose out to the ears, then run your index fingers up the sides of his nose and out to the eyebrows. Run your thumbs across his closed eyelids. Then do it harder.

Next, rub your fingers in gentle circles at his temples. When your contented Virgo is close to falling asleep, gently turn him over and start working your way down his back. Read the massage tips starting with the chapter on Sagittarius to know how to massage the lower part of the body.

Note: Every sign has its opposite sign, and in Virgo's case it is Pisces. Since Pisces rules the feet, on the next massage, start from the bottom up. Read Pisces for some tips on how to treat your lover to the art of Reflexology.

WHERE IS THAT ROMANTIC GETAWAY?

Virgo is a purist when it comes to just about everything and that includes his physical and spiritual self. He's always trying to become more spiritual, more pure (remember his sign is the virgin)…to get in tune with his higher being. Going off to a yoga retreat where you can meditate, commune with nature, eat healthy foods and really unwind would be nirvana for this lover.

Fortunately, most of these retreats are situated in beautiful spots -- in misty forests or on the shores of glistening lakes, etc.

Nicest of all is their cost, they're usually less than half of what you'd pay at a luxury health resort. Of course you won't get satin sheets and saunas either, but your man will find something very cleansing to the spirit about getting back to basics.

You'll discover these places advertised in most of the magazines in your health food market. You will soon be checking out the nearest natural food market so that you can impress your Virgo with how organic the dinner is, won't you??

Imagine you are now with your lover walking hand in hand through the woods. You both arose early that morning and joined a soothing yoga class, stretching both muscles and mind.

Now you have separated yourselves from the others and have disappeared into the woods. The haunting music of an Indian flute can still be heard in the distance. Soon you find your own private spot, and there is nothing but the rustling of leaves to be heard as you both meditate on the surrounding beauty.

Your spiritual energy seems to draw you closer and you reach out to touch hands... the next thing you know you're clinging to each other in the softness of a deep pile of leaves...your lover is untying the string on your white cotton yoga pants...he whispers that he wants to show you what sexual pleasures Tantric Yoga brings...you feel his soft mouth on yours...the filtered sun is dancing behind your closed eyelids...as you totally submit to the moment...as the leaves tumble around you, as...

HOW TO PLEASE VIRGO SEXUALLY.

Around midnight is a good time to bewitch your lover.

We know that Virgo likes everything spick and span, in its place, cleanliness is next to Godliness and so on...but when it comes to sex, your lover has an earthy, down-and-dirty streak that is just waiting to be ignited.

A party for your mouth...

All the lights in the house should be out. Instead of staying in the bedroom, or even in front of the fire, take his hand and gently lead him to the kitchen, taking just enough time to switch on the stereo to something low down and bluesy.

"I've saved a special dessert just for myself," you whisper to him.

When he questions what it is, tell him..."you."

Open the refrigerator door wide and leave it open. You've already changed the color of the light inside to an icy blue.

You may also want to purchase a small strobe light that can sit on the counter, along with a three-colored gel (red, green and blue), that rotates. The effect will be wild and psychedelic. If you like the sound of that, you may prefer to substitute the blues with some heavy metal.

Make sure the shelves of the fridge are filled with glass see-through bowls of different colored fruits. Also tall clear bottles of cranberry juice, apple juice and something sparkling. On the bottom shelf is chocolate mousse cake. Stock a dozen tall cans of whipped cream. The whole picture should look like a party for your mouth.

In the hypnotic blue light of the fridge, slowly remove your lover's clothes while you remain totally dressed. Now tell him to close his eyes and turn him around six times fast. If he's still steady, turn him three more. We want his equilibrium off, which is akin to getting a delightful high. Actually, if you think that's an innovative and inexpensive high, wait till we get to the whipped cream cans!

Pour on the pleasure. . .

Tell him to hold onto the refrigerator door and stare at the blue light. While he's doing this, you quietly pour a bottle of warm, very fine olive oil over his head and down his entire body, while you rub it into his skin. From head to toe. Take your time rubbing it down, down, down his back, along the curve of his thigh, and if you want to stop and explore...the night is young.

Help him to sit down in the puddle of oil on the floor. The first time any man feels oil on his butt, while sitting naked on a kitchen floor, as a flow of cold air from the fridge cools his burning sex, is a memorable moment.

Now let him watch you slowly undress yourself, throwing your clothes with great sluttish abandon into the next room. Then hand him a can of whipped cream and let him use his imagination and the entire can of cream on decorating you.

Whipped to a frenzy...

What remains is an empty can of what is commonly known as "laughing gas" or whippets. By inhaling the last compressed air in the can, your lover will get another incredible high. This is important for Virgo, because it will be easier for him to enjoy every bit of lovemaking once he loses his inhibitions. And if he has other preferences, you may want to ease his tensions with his favorite wine, or whatever, before you get down to serious whipped cream artistry. However, when that finally happens, you can be sure that your lover will use every sense -- touch, taste, sight, smell -- to experience that whipped stuff.

Now it's the time to see what happens when whipped cream and oil merge into what may be your very first gourmet psyche-delic orgasm. I guarantee you'll never find the recipe in a Julia Childs cookbook.

Share the fantasy...

My, my, what goes on in that Virgo lover's fantasy would bring the color to a church lady's cheeks! One of your lover's fantasies is to lose himself in lewdness. To live out all the naughty, disgustingly wonderful things he's seen on the best X-rated films. Therefore, it makes sense that a video camera set up in the bedroom will be a tremendous turn on.

What's more, you're going to mix this particular fantasy with another fantasy of his. That's sado-masochistic love play, with himself in the slave role.

Flash back to the kitchen. . .

Knowing this about him, you might want to begin this role play by spanking him on his oiled round butt. Hard. Let that be a preview for what will take place in the bedroom, in front of the video camera, when you say "action!"

Since I have great faith in your imagination, I won't direct your personal script. Suffice it to say that prim and proper Virgo will love to act the part of your slave...assuming the most erotic positions that will be videotaped for your viewing pleasure. Make sure Virgo knows that if he doesn't obey your instructions, you will spank him. Hard.

It might a good idea for you to keep your private parts clothed and private during this session. Let your lover remain naked and vulnerable.

Note: For the most pleasure, take Olivia's advice and don't let him climax until you have enough video tape to play back.

When you get him excited enough, tell him to make love the

way he always fantasized. Then run the tape and let him watch
what he's only done in front of his own mirror -- when he
dreamed about the woman he now holds in his arms.

LIBRA

SEPT 23 – OCT 22

RULING PLANET: VENUS

MASCULINE, POSITIVE, AIR SIGN

EROTIC DRIVE: TO HARMONIZE

COLORS: PASTEL BLUES, PINKS, PALE YELLOW

GEM: OPAL

PASSION FLOWER: BEGONIA

MAGIC SCENT: PRIMROSE

METAL: COPPER

HERBS:

Archangel   Burdock   Pennyroyal

*"Eroticism is mystique; that is, the
aura of emotion and imagination
around sex."*

**Camille Paglia
"Sexual Personae"**

Your Libra lover is constantly on a quest; searching for harmony and love. That is why the astrological symbol for this sign is the balance scales... weighing, judging, attempting a perfect balance in an imperfect world.

Yes, this is the beautiful air sign of Libra, and I use the word *beautiful* to describe Libra males too, because everything they do is touched by their incredible sense of the aesthetic.

Your lover knows that life is a lot more appealing with a partner to share it, and so his search for the perfect mate begins at an early age.

Naturally, because they have such deep romantic natures, these men are prone to fall madly in love with love. That's why Libras, more than most, have to watch out for getting married too young. More than one hot-blooded Libra with his head in the clouds and his hot little hand in...oh, well, suffice it to say that many have found themselves going down the aisle when they would have been smarter heading for college,

Libra, ruled by the planet of beauty and love, Venus, tells us that your lover might be handsome, and definitely more than average good looks. What's more, everything about him screams *charming.* His girlfriends' mothers adore him, bosses show him off to clients, wives love having him around for their single girlfriends. He seems to have been born with perfect manners, elegance and the instinct to please.

Note: Pleasing is very important to this man. Sometimes it's too important. Libra just might sacrifice what he really wants, what he really thinks, in order to keep up his reputation as *that great guy.*

Interestingly enough, although he seems like the easy and gentle Prince Charming of fairy tales, some of the most militant men in history have been Librans. Eisenhower for one. Even Hitler and Mussolini had Libra very strong in their charts. So take note ladies, there's a lot of steel under that silk.

But don't worry, nobody is perfect (present company excluded) so lets take a closer look at the man you've chosen to warm your bed.

WHAT TURNS HIM ON?

All our astrological lovers want to be admired, but none more than slightly narcissistic Libra. So the first step is to let him know how exceptional you think he is. Next, because Libra, like Cancer, is usually very close to Mama, make sure that you go out of your way to be nice to her. And when Olivia says out of your way, that means take luggage if you have to!

Important note: Because your lover's relationship with his mother is so complex, there will be times when they argue and he comes to you to unburden his inner feelings about *that witch*. Never, never make the mistake of talking against her. Just listen and nod sympathetically. Sooner or later (and it will probably be sooner because Libra hates to stay angry) they will kiss and make up. If you've been talking against her, guess who's going to inherit that broomstick?

Oh yes, it doesn't hurt to be subtly aggressive. Even though Libra loves the idea of love, sometimes he's just too passive about this whole seduction business -- a little too used to having everything fall into his lap -- so since he's not always the pursuer, you might have to stir that old pot to get it to boil.

WHAT TURNS HIM OFF?

Giving Libra a woman who likes to clear the air with a good, old-fashioned, down and dirty name-calling fight would be like putting pollen under an asthmatic's nose. Libra must have harmony in his surroundings. He can become physically ill if caught in the midst of negative vibes. Before that happens though, he will bend over backwards to keep the peace.

Also, as I told you, this man is the very epitome of fine taste and breeding. He intuitively knows the right shirt to wear with the right pants. Probably a combination that less confident souls wouldn't dare try. So take two steps back and look at yourself.

Run in your stocking? Lipstick on your teeth? Dirt under your fingernails? Chewed fingernails?? You might as well have a venereal disease because that's how attractive you'll seem to this lover. Your man notices all the details, so you should do the same.

IS LIBRA A ONE WOMAN MAN?

Yes, but you have to catch him first. Flirting is foreplay to Libra and he loves to tease, pull back, tease a little more, pull back...are you becoming seasick?

Of course, since your lover doesn't like anything too overt, it's perfectly fine to give him a delicious taste of his own medicine. So tease, dangle that red juicy apple, and when he gets worked up enough to take a big bite...gotcha!

DO YOU HAVE WHAT IT TAKES TO SEDUCE LIBRA?

It's honesty-therapy time. Are you the type of female who goes to the ballet and titters behind her program at the bulge in the male dancer's tights? tsk, tsk. Have you been known to turn catatonic at the opera? Are you in your element when bowling a spare? You get the idea, don't you? Libra loves everything having to do with the arts, traditional and avant-garde, and he wants someone who can really appreciate it with him. So, if you'd rather be square dancing than watching Swan Lake...

WHAT COLOR TURNS HIM ON?

Indigo blue works magic for Libra. Because your lover is so sensitive to beauty, you can delight him by finding that special color in a myriad of beautiful and unusual objects...like Chinese fans, antique prints, Spanish shawls, etc. Whatever colors you use in your home or in your wardrobe, think in subtle hues, forget the gilt and glitter, and leave shocking pink shirts and lime tights for somebody else's fantasy.

WHAT'S HIS WORST FAULT?

Some Librans have been accused of having splinters in their beautiful butts, simply from sitting on the fence too long. These men are always so busy looking at the big picture, judging, doing their own inimitable balancing act, that it can take them forever to make a decision.

They have also been accused of being lazy. Happily, Olivia will be a lot kinder. The truth, as I prefer to see it, is that they tend to procrastinate. If the affliction is severe, it may seem at times that your lover just can't get his act together. That thesis he's been talking about since 1992 never seems to get written, the wachya-ma-call-it that's falling apart in the kitchen never gets fixed and so on.

Also, Libra loves to be loved. Now you might think that's an endearing trait. Well, every up has its down side, and in this case it means they're tempted to be not quite as honest as they could be. They tend to sugar-coat the bitter truth in order not to offend anybody.

What's your lover really thinking? Do you really know?

DOES HE HAVE A TEMPER?

As you know by now, Librans hate arguments and confrontations. So be sure to let your lover know that he can say what's on his mind without worrying that you're going to throw him off balance with a well-aimed plate.

Of course, if you push Libra too hard for too long, you may find yourself in a first row seat at a rare performance of: "LIBRA BLOWS HIS COOL." Many in this sign seem to gravitate towards the legal profession. So in an argument, expect Libra to defend his case very well. He's done his research, his facts are flawless, and you won't have a leg to stand on.

The one thing that can raise Libra's ire as nothing else is when his sense of right is wronged. Remember that the symbol of this sign is the scales of justice, and Libra will fight like the warrior he really is to defend a principle.

John Lennon was a Libra dedicated to fighting the good fight, upholding his ideals, loving beauty, always trying with his words and music to make the world a better place.

IS LIBRA GOOD WITH CHILDREN?

Yes, this sign of balance and harmony is a good father. The only flaw in their parenting skills is that they tend to spoil their offspring. It's no doubt their desire to keep harmony in the home and "what the hell, give Mikey the lollipop even though he's had three and it's five minutes to dinner."

Your lover is also the last one in line when it comes to disciplining the little darlings. In the case of Libra, it's more like a really stern: "Just you kids wait until your mother gets home!"

However, make sure, should you marry this man, that you discuss the rearing and unspoiling of your children. If you let Libra have his way, by the time they're terrifying teenagers, they will be a scary handful for both of you.

WHAT DOES LIBRA CALL HOME?

Your lover, with his innate sense of beauty, manages to create a beautiful home without seeming to try.

He likes a feeling of airy space around him, so if he can afford it, he might prefer a large house to an apartment. But wherever he lives, it won't be overdressed with furniture. He'd much prefer his eye to rest on miles of gleaming parquet floors...or white carpet.

Plus he prefers to have his furniture comfortable as opposed to just "the latest" in design. That means you won't be seeing those incredibly expensive modern chairs that resemble torture instruments from the 17th century. Instead, there will be lightly colored furniture and a large, beautiful billowy sofa in which you can both sink and hide away from the world.

You'll love the talent Libra has with decorating. He can put the strangest combinations together and, suddenly, they just seem to harmonize.

HOW DO YOU DRESS FOR A LIBRA?

Ruled by Venus, your lover is one of the most romantic of men. He idealizes women and sees them as fragile creatures to be loved and protected. Of course, if you look as beautifully feminine as that famous Libra, Catherine Deneuve, so much the better. The rest of us must be satisfied with creating the perfect illusion.

The blue indigo flowing skirt you bought is perfect to stroke his imagination. A fragile chiffon blouse, velvet capes, fabrics that arouse his admiration and his senses.

Now take a tip from your lover and be fairly eclectic in the way you dress. In the same way that your Libra appreciates the unexpected in modern art, he'll be captivated with that lovely antique satin blouse worn with a pair of well-worn 501's.

RECIPE FOR A PERFECT EVENING.

Libra rules the kidneys and so your lover should drink a lot of spring water. Purchase the best bottled water and be sure to keep gallons on hand.

The cell salt for Libra is Sodium Phosphate. When your lover (whose symbol is the balance scales) becomes off balance emotionally due to the callousness of society or the pettiness of his co-workers -- or just a damn traffic tie-up! -- be sure he's getting enough of his cell salt in the following foods: wheat, rice, peas, carrots, pears, beets, celery, corn, spinach, kale, strawberries, figs, apples.

Libra rules the kidneys, and there are some herbs to help keep him healthy. Thyme and fennel are good Libran herb to be used in your cooking. Burdock is also an important herb to help strengthen the kidneys.

Don't be shy about asking the people in your health store about herbs. They'll tell you the best way to prepare them, and whether they can be served as teas, like Pennyroyal, which can be brewed for your Libra as a particularly warming and soothing tea.

FIRST STEP:

This is going to be a little more complicated than putting some shrimps on the barbie. You must start with the table setting. Libra loves beauty, remember? The way the table looks (the colors are very important) and the way in which the food is served can either inspire his erotic appetite or totally destroy it.

Put away the paper napkins and lay out the linen ones you hate to iron. Make sure the tablecloth is just as sparkling clean and lovely. Splurge on some pretty napkin holders. Candles? Of course, along with fresh flowers.

SECOND STEP: VENUS CONSUMME

This is the easy way to serve an elegant consummé without doing all the work:

1 quart of canned consummé
1/2 cup dry white wine or sherry
1/3 cup chopped carrots
1/3 cup chopped onion
1/3 cup chopped celery
1/3 cup chopped Daikon
1/3 cup fresh, chopped
green beans
2 tbs butter
salt and pepper
Minced parsley

First, buy a gourmet brand of consummé in the supermarket. Duck bouillon is a Julia Childs favorite. Then, put a cup of the consummé in a saucepan, simmer the above ingredients, except for the wine or sherry, until tender but not browned. Just before you serve, pour the rest of the consummé into the simmered vegetables and follow with "dribbling" in the sherry or wine until you get just the right heavenly taste.

NOTE: You can serve the consummé elegantly in individual soup cups or in a great old-fashioned tureen.

THIRD STEP: SENSUOUS SHRIMP

2 tbs olive oil
1 small onion chopped
1 large or 2 small cloves garlic, minced
1 can (16 oz) tomatoes with their juice
1 tbs red wine vinegar
1 1/2 lbs. shrimp, shelled and deveined
1/2 red bell pepper, cut in thinstrips
Cayenne to taste

Be careful to buy your shrimp in an immaculately clean place, and then take care to wash and de-vein them thoroughly.

Put oil in a large heavy skillet. Sauté onion and garlic until both are soft but not browned, about 10 minutes. After you've broken up the tomatoes with a wooden spoon, add them (along with the juice) and simmer the mixture for about 10 minutes. Add vinegar, red pepper and shrimp, stir thoroughly until the shrimp is coated with the sauce. Add cayenne (about 1 1/2 teaspoons), cover and simmer for 10 more minutes. Serve with or over rice.

NOTE: You don't have to settle for that old tired minute rice either. Or dependable old brown rice. Visit a natural food market and you'll be amazed at the varieties available.

FOURTH STEP: TEASING SANGRIA

3 cups dry red wine
1 lemon cut into slices
3 cups spring water
ice cubes
sugar to taste

This is a nice change from white wine with dinner and goes along with the Spanish recipe above. Combine these ingredients and pour the results into a pretty glass pitcher and serve it cold with the meal.

FIFTH STEP: SUBMISSIVE SALAD

1 bunch Spinach, thoroughly washed and cut into bite sized
    pieces
2 medium tomatoes chopped
1 cucumber sliced
1/2 cup Cheddar cheese
1/2 cup croutons

Note: This might be overkill. After all, you've sated your lover with soup, shrimp and rice, so you can skip the salad if you want. However, if he's mentioned that he must have his greens every day, keep it chilled in the refrigerator until ready to serve. Then pour your favorite dressing over it, mix thoroughly, and serve with the main course.

INTERMISSION:

Your lover might want to stretch his legs at this point. Stroll into the living room where you can impress him with that over-priced new art book you picked up. Of course, you asked him a while back what art appealed to him, didn't you? Whether it was French Impressionism, or Egyptian sculpture, or Disney cartoons, that's the book that should be lying on the coffee table right now.

Then, before he gets sleepy...wake up his taste buds with this dessert.

SIXTH STEP: PARFAIT EROS

You can make this well in advance and be relaxed enough to enjoy it later.

1/2 cup sugar
1/4 cup water
2 egg yolks, well beaten
1 1/2 cups heavy cream
1 tsp vanilla
1 tbs instant coffee, decaf
1/2 square (1/2 ounce) grated unsweetened chocolate
confectioners sugar

Combine water and sugar in saucepan and simmer, stirring gently until the sugar is dissolved. Bring to a boil and cook until syrup spins a thread when dropped from tip of spoon. Fold in egg yolk mixture, then fold in the chocolate, coffee and vanilla. Mix well and spoon into parfait glasses. Cover tops with foil and freeze until firm.

Whip the remaining cream with one tablespoon of confectioner's sugar. When ready to serve, remove the foil and top the parfaits with sweetened whipped cream.

WHAT'S THE MOST SENSITIVE PART OF HIS BODY?

Libra rules the kidneys and although that's not the preferred place to start a massage, it's certainly the general area we want as a landing site.

Since Libra's opposite sign is Aries, let's begin by gently stroking his head (Aries rules the head, remember?) which at this moment, is lying securely in your loving lap. As you gently move your fingers in a circular motion on either side of his temples, you'll be erasing every negative thought. Leaving only wonderfully R-rated visuals of you.

For the best way to give your lover a full body massage, read the massage techniques in Aries through Leo and from Sagittarius to Aquarius.

Don't forget to have perfumed candles burning while you're treating Libra to this massage. Like everything Libra likes, make the scent light, subtle and captivating.

WHERE IS THAT ROMANTIC GETAWAY?

It's April, you're in like, love or lust...where's the most romantic place you can go? Paris, of course. Actually, it doesn't matter what month it is, when you're in love in Paris, it is *always* April.

Libra, the eternal romantic and art lover, will be in his element in the city of lights. Surrounded by the finest museums, every building a masterpiece of architecture, the air filled with the sighs of a thousand lovers.

If you have the francs to afford it, you've booked a room at the elegant Crillon Hotel or the George V on the *rive droit*. But if you're counting *centimes,* then try one of the old and charming *rive gauche* hotels where you have to run up four flights and risk cardiac arrest as you race to beat the timed light switches on each floor. Many an *affair-magnifique* has begun in the dark of a French hotel landing.

Wherever you are, you will wake to the Parisian sun smiling at you behind closed shutters. The maid brings you hot *croissants,* swirled butter in little white tubs and huge steaming cups of *cafe au lait.* You snuggle down next to your lover in the big feather bed. Today you will repeat a time-honored tradition and stroll hand-in-hand along the waters of the Seine, watch the *bateau-mouche* sail by, and then sit at Les Deux Maggot cafe and watch the world stroll by. But for now, the bed is much too warm and your lover smells much too delicious to leave.

"Je t'aime" you whisper, trying out your French.

He doesn't answer...but his actions speak a thousand words

...all with the perfect accent...as he reaches for you...he kisses
you...you sigh deeply as his head disappears under the feather
coverlet...and...*vive l'amour!*

HOW TO PLEASE LIBRA SEXUALLY.

What I know, and what you might have discovered by now, is
that your man is a terrible tease.

Libra loves to bring that simmering pot to a boil and just
when the bubbling starts, he pours a little cold water on the mix
and starts all over again. Next to teasing, he loves being teased --
that means he's a great audience for watching the art of seduction (with you as the beautiful seductress, of course).

Let's set the stage.

If you've been taking notes, you realize by now that no sign is
more sensitive to his surroundings than Libra. So if you can't go
to Paris...go for the satin sheets. The sensuality of satin cannot
be underestimated. You slide. You slither. You squirm more
deliciously on shiny satin sheets than on any other kind.

Now please use your head when choosing the color. If you
have dark skin, you'll look more enticing when lying on a pastel
background. Light skinned females should stick to royal reds
and deep cobalt blues.

Any other ideas spring to mind in the way of sinful bedroom
luxury? A mirrored wall is a very smart investment. Or how
about a deep-piled Floaki white wool rug on the bed? You can
nestle down in it like a lioness in the deep grass, just waiting
for something, tender juicy and delicious to eat.

Your candle burns at both ends...

Yes, I know that you look fabulous in candlelight, we all do
darling, that's why Olivia always recommends more than one
candle...more than a few...and enough to make your bedroom
look as though something spiritual and magical is about to be
performed.

Important note: make sure the candlelight is subdued. Buy
candle holders to shield the harsh flame and diffuse it through
color. Brass candle holders that are filigreed, letting the light
cast wonderful shadows on the walls, are also exciting. Should
you use perfumed candles? Of course!

Now that you've got him in your tender trap, you're going to

give Libra a healthy dose of his own medicine -- you're going to
tease him to death. Remember, teasing takes a very good sense
of timing. And this time it's going to be *you* stirring *his* pot.

All this fun begins after his usual, artful, teasing foreplay.
He's touched you, kissed you, played serious games with your
body for endless amounts of time, while the music played and
the candles burned. Now, his sex is ready to explode and you
know that one touch with your finger can trigger it...

Don't touch...

Instead reach for the bottle of heated massage oil. It's warm
and fragrant in your palm. Now make a circle with your thumb
and index finger and very lightly, like butterfly wings, gently
stroke his hardness up and down until you feel the electricity...
keep stroking very lightly, while the invisible sparks (very real
if you do it right) move between his skin and your fingertips.

Only the deadest man won't be moaning and writhing on the
bed. He's not used to being teased and what he's now experiencing is a delicious and tormenting sensation.

Bring him to the crest of that incredible orgasm that's waiting
just behind his next gasp and then...

Don't do it. . .

Instead slip, slidin' away on the satin, telling your burning
Libra that you have a surprise for him.

Just reach down under the bed, or under the pillow, and take
out that adorable little vibrator you picked up on your last trip
to the village. At the buzzzzz of the vibrating motor, your lover
will be shocked and delighted. Especially when he sees that you
intend to use it on him.

Again, remembering to do everything slowly, move the vibrator towards him and barely touch the inside of his thigh. This
alone might be enough to make him let go. If it looks that way,
immediately take it away. If he can stand the exquisite agony,
then continue a little...then stop...a little...while you kiss him a
little...now ask him how bad he wants to come...and when he
tells you, move the vibrator to either penetrate him or caress
him.

Note: Don't feel guilty now for postponing your lover's pleasure. As a matter of fact, Tao philosophy tells us that the less
often a man ejaculates, the longer he's likely to live. It's a belief

that many older, sexually active men follow, and these men are able to make love many times a day and enjoy inner orgasms without ejaculation. Inner orgasms, you ask bewildered? That's right, my dear. The wonders of sexual variety never cease!

Pick up a book on Eastern philosophies and you'll be very surprised, and educated by what you learn about the art of erotica.

If you care to share this knowledge with your lover (unless of course he's 20-years old and has the stamina of a bull!) you may also enjoy teaching him how to hold back his ejaculation. The ancient Chinese technique is to have him use his fore and middle fingers of his left hand...to exert pressure on the point between scrotum and anus for about three seconds while taking a deep breath.

Now back to present pleasure.

Share the fantasy...

Are you ready for more insights into your lover's psyche? Well, your man is a bit of an exhibitionist and loves to be admired. (If you do have a mirrored wall in your bedroom, your Libra will take a lot of pleasure and a lot of time to admire both of you in it.)

Now before I tell you about his next inclination, you'd better have something to bite on. No, not him! It's just that this man also has a deep-rooted and totally unconscious desire for crossdressing. Now that doesn't mean that the next time he admires your teddy he really wants to be parading around in it.

I'm not saying that he's homosexual, only that we all have dark and strange urges that lie beneath the surface. Sometimes it's exciting to satisfy those urges with your lover. How far you go depends on how close you are, and because that kind of trust takes years to build...here's a fun game to explore in the meantime.

When actress Demi Moore posed for the cover of Vanity Fair with her gorgeous naked body painted from head to sole, she was the result of an artist's vision. Well, my dear, you are about to get your creative juices off, so to speak. At the same time, your lusty Libra will be experiencing a bit of the feminine mystique which he fantasizes within himself.

Again, please understand that this is perfectly normal behavior for Libra males who were born under the symbol of the scales of justice, and are constantly searching for the balance within themselves.

This little game can also satisfy your lover's exhibitionist flair by posing him in front of a mirror, lit by a real black light while you paint him with DayGlo paint.

If you were around in the sixties, you might have had your own body painted in psychedelic rock clubs. Cannabis set the mood. The lights and iridescent colored paint did the rest.

Imagine letting your brush tease his body from his forehead down. I would love to see the results of your artistry, and I'm tempted to ask all you mad and crazy Impressionists out there to send in photos. Hmmm, it would be sort of fun to have an "Olivia's Art Exhibit" featuring your imagination. But, I'll leave you to your privacy while you paint your own fantasies on your Libra lover's body. An exotic abstract? An erotic primitive?

I assure you, when it comes to combining art and sex, a Libra man will be up for anything...

SCORPIO

OCT 23 – NOV 21

RULING PLANETS: MARS/PLUTO

FEMININE, NEGATIVE, WATER SIGN

EROTIC DRIVE: TO DOMINATE

COLOR: PURPLE

GEM: TOPAZ

PASSION FLOWER: CARNATION

MAGIC SCENT: GERANIUM

METAL: STEEL

HERBS:

Scabius   Wormwood   Bur reed

*"Nor did their sex ever seem to have a
beginning, a middle, an end. They
helped each other to deep-purple
portions of sex, portions that seemed
to begin and end nowhere."*

**Erica Jong
"Parachutes & Kisses"**

Mysterious, brooding, passionate, hypnotic. These are the
undercurrents raging in the depths of magnetic Scorpio.
   Ruled by Pluto, your lover belongs to a water sign that is one
of the most complex in the zodiac. Make sure that he's all
grown up before you consider signing his name after yours. No
matter how witty, charming and fantastic in bed he may be...the
last thing you need is a Scorpio lover who stopped growing
emotionally around the age of eleven.
   You see, if Scorpio is an evolved soul who's been around the
cosmos a few times, then you have found a man of tremendous
control and purpose. But if he still has many karmic lessons to
learn, then be prepared for a lover of dizzying extremes -- one
who can rise to great heights and be equally capable of crashing
to zero.
   It has been said that Scorpio is either a saint or a sinner.
Consider that the scorpion is the only animal capable of sting-
ing himself to death with his own tail. That aptly illustrates the
dangerous extremes to which this lover can go. However, don't
dwell on that too long or you may decide that spending
Saturday nights with a video of "Harry Met Sally" isn't so bad
after all.
   Think about this instead: your passionate lover is also symbolized by the eagle. Muse on the incredible imagery of the
Phoenix rising from the ashes and regenerating itself. No matter
how self-destructive he's been, your Scorpio is always capable

of being reborn, of soaring above what seemed like total disaster.

But whether he's on top of the world or crushed beneath it, expect this fascinating and maddening lover to do nothing halfway.

It takes a lot of living to satisfy Scorpio's tremendous appetite for experiences of *every* kind...and it takes quite a woman to satisfy his insatiable hunger for love and sex. This sign is known as the sign of sex, were you aware of that? If you have a naughty little half-smile on your face right now, I guess you knew it only too well. If not, just consider it justice for never winning the Lottery! It all means that your Scorpio won't be satisfied with a half-way performance from you, so if you've got what it takes, be ready to give it all. Followed by encore after encore!

Then again, all this man has to do is to look deeply into your eyes with that hypnotic smoldering gaze of his. You know the one...it not only possesses you, but buys the lease on your soul for the next hundred years. It was probably just that look that made Elizabeth Taylor marry her famous Scorpio, Richard Burton, twice!

WHAT TURNS HIM ON?

A woman who doesn't hold back in life, who's ready to taste every pleasure, every sensation. Because that's exactly what Scorpio wants to do. Plus he's not easily impressed. You're going to have to talk more than a good game to keep his interest.

Also, Scorpio's privacy is very important to him. He appreciates a woman who keeps the details of your intimate moments for just the two of you. Oh, so you think your relationship is fascinating enough to interest Oprah? I suggest you restrain yourself. The more Scorpio feels he can trust your sense of discretion, the more likely he is to confide in you.

Also, a clever female who tells Scorpio that he's so "deep" and "so difficult to really know" will be telling this enigmatic man just what he wants to hear.

WHAT TURNS HIM OFF?

The last thing your lover wants is a woman whose goal is to reform him. You want him to cut out cigarettes or drinking? Do

his manners leave something to be desired? And couldn't he
just iron that damn shirt and remove the Sushi stains before he
meets your mother?

Scorpio will interpret your tender concern as a brutal attack --
and when this man thinks he's being attacked, watch out, he
fights back ferociously. Take Olivia's advice and let him come
around in his own way, in his own time. Suggest it once.
Suggest it twice, and then drop it. The minute you begin to
sound like a missionary, or worse, a nag, nag, nag, will be the
end of your relationship.

Remember, too, that your lover is very secretive, to the point
of sometimes being downright mysterious. That's exactly the
image of himself that he wants to create. He likes dark corners
and shadowed crevices in which to hide. You're just going to
have to bite your lip and wait until he confides in you. Trying
to dig into his past will only annoy him and frustrate the sweetness out of you.

IS SCORPIO A ONE-WOMAN MAN?

Yes, but you'll pay dearly for the pleasure. If you haven't discovered it by now, your lover is *very* jealous and extremely possessive. If he hasn't branded his initials on the inside of your
thigh, it isn't because he hasn't fantasized it.

This is definitely not the man to play head games with -- you
know the kind -- when you flirt a little at a party to make your
lover jealous? Don't play those games, because with this man,
you just might bite off more than you can chew. He'll get even
with you and it won't be pretty!

With Scorpio, it's much smarter to let him know in every way
that you're his woman and not even an incredible stud with
Kevin Costner's mouth, Billy Crystal's humor, Billy Joel's
rhythm and Ross Perot's credit limit can get close to you.

So, lie a little.

DO YOU HAVE WHAT IT TAKES TO
SEDUCE SCORPIO?

If you can satisfy Scorpio's emotional and sexual needs then
you can wrap him around your little finger. But that's not as
easy as it sounds. You have to love sex as much as he does, and

to Scorpio, sex is just a *little* more important than breathing. He also wants a woman who will experiment in bed. Are you prepared to travel down foreign roads without censuring yourself -- to explore your own hidden depths? No holding back?

Now don't think Scorpio *only* wants a woman in the bedroom. I mean, he loves sex in the kitchen, bathroom, foyer and closets, too.

The point is: what goes on in your mind is also as important to Scorpio. Unlike Gemini, who is often satisfied knowing a little about a lot of things, this man goes to the intellectual core.

One of his deepest interests is the occult. That takes in the vast world of psychic phenomenon including telepathy, astral projection, clairvoyance etc. The unknown and mysterious fascinate Scorpio and he wants to know the "why" of everything. Actually, there isn't anything this lover doesn't want to penetrate to its very core...beginning with you.

WHAT COLOR TURNS HIM ON?

Vibrant magenta portrays the passion that is so very like Scorpio. Your lover doesn't respond so well to weak pastels, so use bold colors, especially magenta, as an accent color in your wardrobe and home. Actually, his tastes encompass reds and purples, too. Not lavender, mind you, but rich, powerful, sensual purple.

He also responds to the starkness of red and black. It's dramatic. It's straight to the point. Just like the man himself.

WHAT'S HIS WORST FAULT?

The less mature Scorpio male (you know, the one Olivia warned you to stay away from) drowns his troubles in sex, drugs or alcohol. Of course, if he uses sex as a sort of holistic medicine and gets it from only one family doctor, namely you, it might not be so dangerous. But an immature Scorpio who hasn't learned to control his passions tends to go off the deep end. This is the fellow who burns his candle at both ends and then wonders why there's a permanent room reserved for him in the intensive care ward.

All of the above is why it's so important that you make sure your lover is fairly mature before losing your heart to him.

Now comes that question of stubbornness. He's a hard man to talk to when he gets his mind fixed on something. Happily, he's smart, and intuitive, so try to have patience until he swallows that false pride and sees the light.

DOES HE HAVE A TEMPER?

You know better than to nag about his faults, right? Then hopefully, it won't be you who will light the fuse.

Unlike other men who "blow up" and then forgive and forget, Scorpio *never* forgets. Remember the sting of a scorpion can be deadly.

The first sign of his temper is sarcasm that goes straight for your jugular. You'll be hurt, your feelings will be seriously wounded. Will that be enough to satisfy your lover? Oh no, now Scorpio will take his phone off the hook, cancel all business meetings and get to plotting how to *really* get even.

Since this man has the uncanny ability to know exactly where your Achilles heel is -- *before* he even knows the location of your birthmark -- expect no mercy. That's why it's important to show him that vindictiveness accomplishes nothing and that communication can move mountains. How do you show him that? By really believing it yourself, for starters. The only problem is that when he's upset, your lover falls into a smoldering silence that's really difficult for the average female to break through.

So you shouldn't have any trouble all!

You'll also find out that Scorpio can be enraged on your behalf. Think twice before you tell him that someone insulted you in the subway, or, heavens forbid, touched your flesh. He'll be off to "take care of him" before the poor nerd can even draw up a will.

IS SCORPIO GOOD WITH CHILDREN?

He makes a caring parent but tends to be too strict. Scorpio's natural inclination to dominate, combined with possessiveness, makes the poor little kiddies feel as if Big Brother is watching over their shoulders 24-hours a day.

So induce your lover (soon to be husband?) to lighten up. Also, explain to him that the surest way of keeping his children close to him, and really loving him when he's old and gray, is to give them freedom…let them go.

By the way, let him know that works like magic in the adult female arena, too.

WHAT DOES SCORPIO CALL HOME?

Unlike Libra, who likes his home light and airy, the place Scorpio calls home tends to be dark and womb-like.

Could this be a manifestation of your lover's secretive nature?

Fabrics are important to his surroundings. He likes rich textures, like brocades and velvets. Lush, sensuous. Think about surprising him with a black velvet smoking jacket for Christmas, or do it for just the erotic fun of it.

Also, since he likes leather, don't be surprised to find leather furniture in the living room and Heaven knows what in leather in the bedroom. After all, this is the most sexual sign in the zodiac, and when it comes to the bedroom, your man's intense erotic imagination will no doubt be seen…and probably felt as well.

I thought it might be inspiring for you to know what the Kama Sutra has to say about the ideal setting for love. Of course, your man isn't expected to furnish this extravagantly sensual setting, but its exotic flavor might well have been written with a Scorpio in mind:

"The abode should ideally be situated near some water and divided into different compartments for different purposes. If possible it should be surrounded by a garden and contain inner and outer rooms. The main room should be balmy with rich perfumes and contain a bed, soft, agreeable to the sight, covered with a clean cloth, low in the middle part, having garlands and bunches of flowers upon it, a canopy above it, and two pillows, one at the top and another at the bottom. There should be a sort of couch, and at the head of this a stool on which should be placed fragrant ointments, perfume and flowers."

HOW DO YOU DRESS FOR A SCORPIO?

Like Leo, they have a flair for the dramatic and they like their women to stand out in a crowd.

So put away the dresses with those sweet little Peter Pan collars. The preppy look is death with this man. He doesn't want a little girl. The only woman who interests him is one who is totally female. Instead, think in terms of clothes that don't whisper but shout, "I love every minute of being beautiful, seductive, intelligent, erotic and yours!"

What delicious pleasure for your Scorpio to see every male in the room salivating over you -- while he knows that he, and only he, will be taking you home. Naturally, that doesn't mean you have to think in terms of dressing flashy in any way --just look sophisticated, sexy, feminine and gorgeous. That's simple enough, isn't it?

RECIPE FOR A PERFECT EVENING.

Your lover is a true sybarite, someone who loves to indulge the pleasures of his senses. That means that he's just a boy who can't say "no" especially when it comes to food and drink. He has a tendency to overindulge both these pleasures. Keep that in mind when serving and especially when pouring.

Like most of his tastes, he prefers exotic, dramatic foods. Lobster newburg, Indian curries, etc. It's worth repeating though, you must get Scorpio to learn to eat more sensibly. Those heavy "snacks" at one in the morning are fine when he's nineteen but dangerous when he's forty. At either age, overeating often shows up in his bad complexion. However, to be truthful, I must add that Richard Burton, whom we mentioned earlier, was a Scorpio whose bad complexion somehow only added to his macho appeal.

The cell salt for Scorpio is Sulphate of lime.

Here are some of the foods that contain this cell salt and are very healthy in Scorpio's diet: Kale, prunes, turnips, radishes, leeks, garlic, cauliflower, asparagus, fresh coconut and blueberries.

Scorpio needs the right herbs in his diet so that he can rid himself of impurities in his system. Blackberry leaves, blessed thistle, horse radish (no, you don't have to serve this with gefilte fish!), and leek all are beneficial for your lover.

When you invite your Scorpio to dinner, arrange to have some other interesting company there, too. He likes fun people when he's dining -- along with a glass of wine, or two or three.

FIRST STEP:

Your lover's imagination is so intense that you really could entertain him in a bare room and he would still get turned on. All this man needs is you and his mind. But to feed that incredible mind, along with his belly, make the decor as colorfully exotic as possible.

The menu is Indian, so how about visiting your favorite Indian shop, or a shop that sells inexpensive Indian gifts? There are some of these boutiques in every city. Pick up an Indian madras tablecloth, a brass candlestick holder, Indian pillows on the chairs, etc. One of those miniature Indian elephants decorated with tiny mirrors will make a colorful centerpiece.

SECOND STEP: CURRIED SHRIMP SUBLIME

Serve this dish on a bed of long grained wild rice. A cool Chablis will be appreciated by your Scorpio.

NOTE: If any of the ingredients in these recipes seem unfamiliar, the person in your gourmet market or Indian grocery can help you out. While you're there, pick up some chutney and serve it as a condiment with this dish.

1/4 cup butter
2 large apples, peeled and chopped
2 cloves of garlic minced
1 1/2 cups of milk or coconut milk
1/2 cup chopped celery
1 tbs shredded coconut
3/4 tsp ginger
1/2 tbs sugar
1 tbs curry powder
1 tsp whole wheat flour
1 tsp salt
1/4 pepper
1 tsp minced parsley
2 pounds raw shrimp, shelled deveined
3 cups hot cooked long-grained rice
2 large tomatoes, peeled, chopped
4 large onions chopped

Sauté the onions and garlic in a heavy skillet until golden brown. Then add the milk and bring to a boil. Next add the tomatoes, apples, celery, coconut and ginger. Combine sugar, curry powder, flour, salt and pepper and blend well. Gradually add to mixture in skillet. Add parsley. Simmer and stir until everything is smooth and the vegetables are tender. Add the shrimp and cook 5 minutes more.

THIRD STEP: CUCUMBER COQUETTE

1 cup plain yogurt
1/2 cup water
1 large cucumber (peeled and sliced in 1/4 rounds)
1 tsp salt
1/4 tsp cumin powder
1/4 cup fresh coriander leaves
1/4 tsp cayenne pepper.

In a large bowl mix the yogurt, water, salt and cayenne. Add cucumbers to yogurt mixture. Sprinkle the cumin powder on top. Garnish with coriander leaves.

INTERMISSION:

This dish serves four people, so while your lover and best friends are talking about what an incredible cook you are, slip into the kitchen and bring out the dessert you wisely made earlier in the day.

FOURTH STEP: PROVOCATIVE INDIAN PUDDING

6 cups of milk
3/4 cup rice
1/2 cup raisins
1/4 tsp cardamom powder
1/2 bay leaf
1/2 cup turbinado sugar

In a large saucepan, combine the milk, rice and bay leaf. Cook for about 15 minutes on a high heat, stirring very frequently. Bring to a boil and then lower the heat to simmer for 40 more minutes until it thickens. Remove the bay leaf and add sugar, raisins and cardamon. Refrigerate until it cool, it will thicken while it cools.

WHAT'S THE MOST SENSITIVE PART OF HIS BODY?

Scorpio rules the genital area, but with this high voltage lover, any part of his body that you touch will cause underground explosions. So to arouse your Scorpio in a way that he won't soon forget...try the low-lighting, erotic massage Olivia suggests for the other signs, too. Don't forget the mood music, perfumed candles, fruit, and give him the softest spot in the house after yourself.

The only problem with volatile Scorpio is being able to *finish* the massage. If you start at the head, there's a good change that you'll never get to the knees. And if you start at the feet, just try reaching the shoulders. Oh no, somewhere in-between is that magnetic field that will be drawing you closer. And I warn you now, there's no use resisting the power of Scorpio's erotic magnetism...charged with an incredible sexual power...so don't even try.

WHERE IS THAT ROMANTIC GETAWAY?

Now this may sound a little kinky, but that's only because it is. For the next month, tell your lover that you're taking him away *every* weekend. Then find the motel closest to you that features fantasy bedrooms.

Scorpio will love the variety of ravishing you in the exotic interior of an Indian setting one week, in a white on white honeymoon suite the next, or in a black art-deco boudoir with wall-to-wall smoked mirrors. Most of these hideaways for lovers offer water beds, Jacuzzis, etc., everything and anything! It's perfect for the most highly sexed lover in the zodiac and the smiling woman on his arm.

Just imagine both of you in the "Jungle" fantasy room. Here the setting is an exotic display of leopard and tiger skins, with bamboo and rattan furniture.

The waterbed moves gently underneath your bodies. As you stroke his skin with oils, your lover seems to belong to this primitive world. He is a beautiful animal...passionate...always hungry for you. Soon the oil from his body touches yours... again and again...until both of you are glistening in the light of the candles...now your Scorpio moves his fingers to the place he knows so well...and you throw away the last shred of inhibition as you...

HOW TO PLEASE SCORPIO SEXUALLY.

Let the games begin!
No, we're not talking about Olympic sports, but another kind of body, soul and mind game that you're going to love losing.
When you and your Scorpio are relaxing together in your apartment, or his, and pondering the possibilities of a sexually explosive evening...offer your lover a game of chance. Now it is totally up to you which game will stimulate his ego, his competitive spirit and his libido. It can be his favorite game of darts, poker or scrabble. Or perhaps if you're lucky enough to have a pool table, or a rec-room that has one, you may want to shoot a few balls. Naturally, if you do play pool, make sure that only one light hangs above the green felt, and that the rest of the room is in the shadows. Then as you sensuously lean over the table, exposing the line of leg, Olivia promises that you'll be immediately ahead of the game.
The point is, my dear, that you will tell Scorpio whoever loses the game will have to remove his or her clothing. And whichever game you play, *you will definitely lose*. This is a game of strip with all its honorable, horny history. Now let's discuss what you soon will not be wearing.
You should have on your most sexy and alluring underwear in the color of his choice, naturally. Considering Scorpio's erotic tastes, that color would no doubt be black, and if you can get black with red ribbons, so much the better. That must be covered with a pair of tight pants so that you can roll them down inch by inch.
Note: Most erotic films usually make the mistake of removing the clothing too fast. It should be agonizingly slow, never forgetting that it is the ultimate tease.
The first thing you must do is unsnap the top button of your pants and glide back the flaps on either side of the fly. Then let

your hand disappear into the mist for just a moment. Quietly smile into his eyes.

Of course, we musn't forget the possibility of your Scorpio preferring to remove your clothing for you. In that case, just stand still or lie back and allow him the pleasure.

The hourglass.

Time is very important in all great games of skill.

You want time to slow down for this man who's always out competing in the fast world. Perhaps you're lucky enough to have found a Scorpio who knows how to savor the moment, but just to insure the right sensual pace...tell your lover that you're going to play by the clock. He has three minutes to roll your pants or shorts below the hips. There will be penalties for racing the clock. Naturally, Olivia is not going to choreograph his every lascivious move for the next three minutes, how he fills his time will be left up to his imagination.

Turn the hour glass over...

The next three minutes he must get to the knees, while you again slip your fingers into your panties, into the mist.

Turn the hour glass over...

At this point, you must sit down on the edge of the bed, or on some overstuffed chair and lean back, slowly bringing your knees up to your shoulders. You do this by lifting your bottom to make the removal of your panties easier. He has three minutes to remove them to your knees, and when he does...

Turn the hour glass over...

So here you are with just the silk of your panties and the one man in the world you want to remove them.

Variations on the theme.

You may want to make the following offer to your Scorpio game player.

Whoever loses will have to masturbate in front of the other.

Of course, you tell him that you're so sure of winning that he'll soon be loving himself before he loves you -- when the

truth is that you have every *intention of losing.* You know that
by masturbating for him, you will be giving him a part of yourself that nobody else sees. And you also know that your Scorpio
loves to dominate. What can be more exciting than to see a
beautiful, submissive you performing the most intimate sexual
act for him?

Share the fantasy...

If you've ever watched a Dracula movie with your lover, then
you know how he reacts when the Count leans over a smooth,
vulnerable neck and takes a little bite. Now we're not saying
that your lover rises to howl at the moon, but if you have the
imagination and sense of humor, create the illusion of a beautiful, mysterious Vampira. You may even don long fingernails,
and buy white rice face power. He may take one look and immediately lose control.

If you're a blonde, your hair will ruin the whole Vampira
effect, so use some dark-colored temporary dye in hair spray
form and turn yourself into Angelica Huston's twin.

Naturally, you will use only Dayglo lights, no candles, and no
white or colored lights. A real Dayglo bulb (black light) will
reflect the white of your face...wonderfully spooky and sensuous.

Now don't go thinking this is too far out...because all great
sex is fantasy brought to life...and nothing is too far out for a
Scorpio.

SAGITTARIUS

NOV 22 – DEC 21

RULING PLANET: JUPITER

MASCULINE, POSITIVE, FIRE SIGN

EROTIC DRIVE: TO EXPLORE

COLOR: SEA GREEN

GEM: TURQUOISE

PASSION FLOWER: RED ROSE

MAGIC SCENT: SAFFRON

METAL: TIN

HERBS:

Agrimony   Solomon's seal   Red Clover

"Why does a gesture, a walk stir your blood? What a mystery this is, desire. The love sickness, the sensitivity, the obsession, the flutter of the heart, the ebb and flow of the blood."

Anais Nin

The last of the fire signs is Sagittarius, ruled by the planet Jupiter. Its symbol is the Archer, half man, half centaur. Perhaps the clue here is that your lover is really half a regular fellow who appreciates the comforts of home -- while the other side of his nature is a freedom loving animal, jumping every fence and bucking every rider.

Ruled by the bountiful planet Jupiter, your man has a profound love of life and a happy-go-lucky attitude that attracts many friends. Few can match his sheer generosity of spirit. His willingness to crawl out of bed at two in the morning to rescue a buddy from some embarassment. He may be among the best friends in the zodiac, and remember, Olivia told you that love affairs beginning as friendships promise longevity.

You've probably discovered that sports is his great pastime, and you'll be nursing more than one torn ligament in your life, not to mention a bruised ego.

You should know that sports just might have something to do with his overall positive outlook. Health specialists tell us that exercising releases testosterones, those little male hormones that build up and cause stress when we turn into couch potatoes. So it might benefit you to become more physical yourself if you're not already -- definitely learn something about soccer, football or whatever his favorite macho-chism may be.

In the end, whether he wins or loses his particular challenge, all that beautiful muscle will eventually come off his playing field and enter *yours*...so you can look forward to many an exciting championship game.

Yes, this man, if he's a positive representative of the sign, should be in superb mental and physical shape. The body of a Sagittarian man who takes good care of what Nature gave him, can be a sight to behold...and to caress. But Sag (that's his nickname, pronounced with a soft "g") is definitely not easy to get, so we had better start creating a strategy.

WHAT TURNS HIM ON?

It may sound perverse, but the lady who really turns on a Sag is the one who seems to do just fine without him. Be independent and never cling. Sag loves his freedom and you must always maintain the illusion that he has it. Tread lightly and he'll never know that you slipped his freedom into your pocket with your car keys.

Do you like the outdoors? Your lover does, and he's usually found on the racquetball court if he's in shape, or just huffing along a country path if he's not. Either way, he doesn't like to feel trapped emotionally or physically. If you can't share his love of the outdoors, then you're leaving the door wide open for that lady with the well-worn Nikes.

Most important, this man is involved in expanding his consciousness on all levels: mental, physical, spiritual. So let him know that you offer him the complete set -- stunning looks, great personality and a fascinating brain. And if you have only two out of three, make sure they're the *last* two.

WHAT TURNS HIM OFF?

Pettiness in any shape or form (even if your shape is a Hollywood 10) will sour this affair. He doesn't have time to sweat the small stuff in life because his mind is usually tuned onto loftier planes. Can you discuss philosophy, religion, the occult? These are three subjects that fascinate your seeker of truth. The sound of wind whistling through a beautiful woman's ears is a definite turn off.

And what sports interest you? Other than chasing him, that is. Your Sag practically lives in the outdoors. Be ready to get acquainted with muscles you never knew you had, try to relate to little furry things in the woods, and for Heaven's sake, don't ask if there's an outlet for your hair dryer on the Appalachian trail!

What you can look forward to are long evenings spent in the

quiet beauty of nature, sitting on the edge of a lake or a mountain top, while your lover waxes philosophical about life's mys-
teries. Since he's always wanting to learn from other people and
really appreciates the exchange of ideas, be prepared to share
your own ponderings on the meaning of life. Is the last deep
thought you read on the side of your herbal tea box? You may
be in trouble. Begin reading a little philosophy. It doesn't matter
if the musings belongs to Kant or Boy George. As long as they're
ideas, Sag will love discussing them.

Oh yes, Sag is the only lover who can compare his lady to a
beautiful horse and get away with it. You see, your lover is
crazy about horses -- from watching them race to owning stables
of his own -- so it may be one of the best left-handed compli-
ments you ever received. Then again, it may not hurt to check
those jeans in a rear view mirror just in case.

IS SAG A ONE-WOMAN MAN?

Happily, you have found one of the most faithful signs in the
zodiac. It's true that he loves his freedom and may not exactly
dash down the aisle. However, once he's made the commitment,
he's in it for the long run.

It's important to know before the concrete sets just how simi-
lar your ideas are on the subject of fidelity. There is a strain of
Sagittarian males who have an avid interest in exploring sexual
partners. If your lover is older, chances are he's satisifed those
energies and is content to settle down. But if he's still young,
with a constant itch he loves to scratch, then talk it out beforehand. You don't need to be surprised by a husband who
believes you had an "open marriage" and then accuses you of
having a closed mind. Many a Sag experiences two marriages in
his lifetime and this is probably one of the reasons why.

As I said, once Sag makes the commitment to be a one-
woman man, everything should be fine. Just be sure you *both*
know that commitment has been made.

DO YOU HAVE WHAT IT TAKES TO SEDUCE SAG?

Well, if your knickname is Ivy because you're famous for
clinging to the man of the moment, then Sag may not be the
right bedmate. This sign hates possessive females and *any*

closed-in feeling. The surest way to see the back of your lover's head as he goes out the door is to:

a. Ask for a commitment before he's even memorized your telephone number.
b. Pout when you see him flirting and make him feel really guilty about it.
c. Pin him down to a set schedule of dating that you've casually written out in blood.

All of the above are guaranteed to trigger his claustrophobia. On the positive side, if you enjoy family ties and togetherness, this relationship may be perfect. Unlike Capricorn, Sag isn't a big one for traditions, but relatives, his blood kin, play a very important part in his life. There may even come a time later on when he accepts the responsibility of caring for elderly relatives. So although you may have to share him from time to time, don't worry, your lover has enough generosity in his nature to go around. Hopefully, you have, too.

WHAT COLOR TURNS HIM ON?

Rich turquoise is a favorite. The combination of this vibrant color combined with brown and white is one of nature's most beautiful. It's the delicious combination of hues on a tropical beach.

Try implementing them in your home or wardrobe or wherever your imagination can conjure. Since your lover loves the outdoors, what better way to bring its beauty inside?

WHAT'S HIS WORST FAULT?

One person's refreshing frankness can be anothers cruel bluntness. If you're very sensitive you may bleed a bit when Sag tells you what he thinks. He's not being mean on purpose, he's just living up to his symbol as the Archer, who shoots the truth into the air and where it lands...watch out! This symbol has also been interpreted erotically as phallic aim and, in that case, you may be sure its destination will be better calculated.

Your lover has more lessons to learn when it comes to generosity of the pocketbook, too. He's already generous with his time and energies, but he may tend to be a tad tight-fisted when it comes to money. So before you begin to clear a shelf for him in the medicine cabinet, the subject of who pays what should be discussed. It's also not a bad tactic to keep telling Sag how generous he is. It's magical how a man can become as wonderful as his lover assures him he is.

Oh yes, Olivia must warn you that Sag is famous for procrastination. Sometimes it's a simple lack of "pulling it together" that's the cause, and at other times he promises too much because he simply wants to please so much.

Lastly, he's so basically optimistic that he's been known to take a chance on just about anything. That means roulette wheels (which isn't a fatal flaw unless he doesn't know when to stop), and a lot of impulsive "let's do it now and kick ourselves in the pants later" behavior. If you can get him to think about his plans before he's up to his neck in consequences, you'll be doing his wallet a big favor.

DOES HE HAVE A TEMPER?

Nothing that a smart woman with a little loving patience and a Baretta can't handle.

Of course, there will be times when you argue, but those storms should pass quickly. Sag is basically very optimistic and he's always sure that love and emotional nourishment is just the medicine to cure your disagreement. Give him a chance...he's usually right.

IS SAG GOOD WITH CHILDREN?

Yes,this man who thirsts for knowledge throughout his life really enjoys his children's quest for the same, beginning with: "Why is the sky blue, Daddy?"

However, there is a period before the adorable questions begin when babies are less interesting to him. Those are the days when Sag parents are busy admonishing: "Don't...don't touch that...didn't I tell you not to touch that!!" It's important that your Sag learns patience to get him through the terrible two's.

WHAT DOES SAG CALL HOME?

Just remember that your man is clean but not always tidy. After all, when you're used to trekking over mountains, you don't worry about a little dust on the fridge or a pleasant mess of magazines spilling over coffee tables. Yes, your lover likes a house that looks lived-in -- in the best sense. One that attracts his friends to plop down on the couch, kick their shoes off and talk into the wee hours of the morning.

Besides comfortable-looking, inviting furniture, probably decorated in warm earth colors, you'll find objects scattered around that he's collected on his travels: masks from Bali, blow guns from the jungles of Peru and so on. A bikini bottom found under a sofa pillow? Well, perhaps it's best not to ask where in his travels he picked up that little momento. Oh yes, don't be surprised if you even discover a pile of books in the john, because reading is such a favorite pastime.

HOW DO YOU DRESS FOR SAG?

This man is down to earth and doesn't want his woman looking artificial. He certainly doesn't want to run his fingers through hair sprayed to the sensual texture of Brillo.

Since you're going to be spending a lot of time in the great outdoors, plan on looking equally natural. That means working to get in shape so that you can look sexy and delicious in jeans, especially as you "bounce" ahead of him on horseback. Get the picture?

Try putting some Indian jewelry in your wardrobe, too -- the turquoise stone set in silver is his favorite color.

Note: Whatever you do, *do not wear fur.* Sag loves all animals and may even be an active animal rights activist. Seeing you wearing animal skins would react on him like a cold, cold shower.

RECIPE FOR A PERFECT EVENING

Sagittarius is, however, a meat and potatoes man. Of course, you should make your dining area as romantic as possible, with the right candles, flowers etc., but the important thing here is he likes food and plenty of it.

When a woman really cares about her lover, she will urge him to eat less meat, and to cut down on both food and liquor. It's a well-known fact that the less we eat, the longer we live. So make him a deal: you won't wear it if he won't eat it. Besides, better health will only make him happier and more agile in the bedroom. What better "nutritional" motivation could there be? Oh yes, get him to curb that sweet tooth of his, too. It's a major vice for most of this sign.

However, Sag does appreciate fresh fruit and vegetables. The cell salt Silica is important to his overall health, and it's found in the skin of fruits and vegetables such as strawberries, figs and prunes. Serve them all and remember to have some frosty beer on hand.

Plan on stopping by your local herbalist to pick up the following herbs. Again, find out what's available as teas and get in the habit of serving your lover healthy herbal teas instead of nerve-jarring caffeine. Red Clover, Burdock, Dandelion and Chicory are all herbs which are beneficial to Sag.

FIRST STEP:

No astrological sign likes to eat in a closed-in space, and that especially goes for don't-fence-me-in Sag. If you're dining area is really tight, how about moving it all into the living room? Open the windows, invite the cool breeze in and your lover will be immediately content. If you can dine *al fresco* on a balcony or terrace, he'll be in heaven.

SECOND STEP: SALACIOUS SOUP

Note: Cut up all the veggies into bite sizes. Naturally, fresh vegetables are preferred, but if you absolutely must, defrost the frozen ones before you put them in the soup.

1 cup corn
1 cup peas
1 cup zucchini
1 cup yellow squash
1 cup tomatoes
1 cup carrots
1 cup celery
1 tbs butter
1 tbs minced garlic
1 cup sliced mushrooms
1 cup onion, diced

1 tbs soy sauce
1 tbs oregano
1 tsp basil
2 tbs honey
6 oz. can tomato paste
Salt to taste
Package of your favorite noodles

Put the first seven ingredients in about 10 cups of water.
Bring to a boil and simmer 20 minutes. Then sauté the next five
ingredients and add to pot. Stir, add herbs, honey, tomato paste
and salt to taste. Serve with cooked noodles.
Note: the soup will be doubly delicious if you use bottled
water.

SECOND STEP: MACHO MEAT LOAF

1 1/2 lbs ground turkey
2 eggs
1/2 cup milk
3/4 cup soft bread crumbs
2 tbs salt
1 tbs oregano
1 tbs Worcestershire
1 tbs Dijon mustard
1 cup chopped mushrooms

Combine turkey, eggs, milk, bread crumbs, salt,
Worchestershire sauce and Dijon mustard in a large bowl. Mix
thoroughly. Spoon into a 9-inch loaf pan.Then make a trough
down the center and spoon in mushroom filling (recipe below).
Next, pat the rest of the meat over filling until the top is
smooth.
Bake 350 F for one hour. Let stand ten minutes before slicing.

MUSHROOM FILLING

2 tbs. butter
1 cup sliced mushrooms

1/2 cup chopped onion
1/2 cup sour cream

Melt butter in skillet. Sauté mushrooms and onion until tender. Let cool. Stir in sour cream.

THIRD STEP: SEDUCTIVE SPUDS

4 white potatoes, boiled
1 cup shredded Cheddar cheese
2 tbs butter, melted
2 tsp salt
1/4 tsp black pepper
1 cup sour cream, room temperature
1 tbs butter
2 tbs chopped green onion

Peel the potatoes and shred coursely into large bowl. Add the cheese and melted butter. Mix lightly. Add the onion, salt, pepper and sour cream. Mix lightly. Turn everything into baking dish and dot with butter. Bake at 350 F for 25 minutes.
Note: It's time to bring out the bottle of good Burgundy.

INTERMISSION:

Let your man stretch his legs. So, far you've given this lucky Sag what he loves most: food that sticks to his ribs -- and a woman who knows how to cook it. Walk around, show him that great heirloom quilt Aunt Sarah sent you, sip more wine, think about the dessert you're going to enjoy after dessert.

FOURTH STEP:

Remember that your lover has a soft spot for a rich dessert, and we certainly aim to please. So you have Olivia's permission to stop by your favorite French patisserie and buy the most sinful chocolate cake in the window. Then pick up some whipped cream and cherries. Serve this with your richest coffee blend.

WHAT'S THE MOST SENSITIVE PART OF
HIS BODY?

Sag rules the hips and thighs and, unfortunately, many of this sign occasionally suffers from sciatica. Your lover probably has built up considerable muscle in his thighs thanks to his love of sports. Along with a sensual full body massage, one of the most wicked ways to drive him wild is to begin while you're simply embracing.

Let your hand drop to his knee, where you caress it for a minute or so. Then, *very* slowly, begin to move your fingertips up his thigh...you reach the top of the thigh and ever-so-lightly, move your fingers to the inside of the thigh and work your way back down towards the knee.

It's surprising anything that feels that good is legal!

WHERE IS THAT ROMANTIC GETAWAY?

Sag is famous for keeping his eye on the horizon and his bags packed. You can expect wonderful adventures with this lover. But for a romantic interlude in the near future, why not choose a ranch, dude or not, to thrill the man who loves horses?

You had better start taking lessons at your local stable if you don't know how to ride. That way, by the time you arrange this little trip, your thigh muscles and derriere will be beyond the screaming stage and simply wimpering. Jane Fonda always advises, "no pain, no gain" and we've all seen pictures of how fabulous she looks astride a horse, as she and her love ride around their quaint little homestead that's about half the size of Montana.

So let's fantasize a little and imagine you and your own cowboy lover on horseback, as you discreetly leave the other guests and take a more private trail.

It's the late in the afternoon when you find a shaded, private spot by a lake. Your Sag is doing what he loves *second* best in the world and that's discussing Life. The sun is setting and he builds a fire. The earthy smell of the horses mixed with the perfume of nature is a heady combination, and it makes you move closer into his warmth. He kisses you and your fingers drop lightly to his knee... and you know where to go from there...

The horses whinny in the twilight...as if knowing that your lover is now about to enjoy what he loves *most* in the world.

HOW TO PLEASE SAGITTARIUS SEXUALLY.

Unlike the woman in love with Aries, who motions for the Ram to be quiet while she orchestrates the scene, your erotic words will tease and tantalize Sag.

Before you're even through with dinner -- at your home, at his, or in a restaurant, start telling him that you know a place where you can make love in the midst of primal nature; that it's going to be an incredible spiritual experience.

Your Sag loves to be turned on by words, and the more graphic they become, the better. If you're shy, just turn down the lights and whisper in his ear. Don't forget to let your fingers explore those taut muscles as you say deliciously naughty things.

Note: Also, don't forget that the ear is still one of the most sensitive erogenous zones. So whispering into your lover's ear will definitely double his pleasure.

What Olivia has in mind for this outdoorsman is a night in the wilds of your bedroom. First you'll need a big, soft rug. A fake bearskin is ideal. And although at any other time I would suggest another Sag to entertain you (Sinatra on the stereo), tonight the music will be a tape of nature sounds. You know how much your man loves the outdoors, and now you are about to give him a totally new and incredible experience -- the ability to enjoy just that in the warmth of your bed. Sex to the sounds of surf crashing and lightening and thunder rumbling across your woofers and tweeters, which then somehow times perfectly with your orgasm to dissolve into bubbling brooks and crickets chirping.

There's a wonderful variety of nature tapes available, so choose whatever sounds transport you.

The soul kiss...

If you've been seeing your Sag for awhile, what I'm about to tell you won't come as a big surprise. He loves oral sex. Mutual oral sex, that is.

There are scores of books on the market that will give you the latest cutting-edge techniques on oral sex. How to hold it, how to taste it, how long to bake it, oops, wrong book! This is one sport in which practice definitely makes perfect.

If you're a beginner, try letting enthusiasm make up for your lack of artistry. You see, most men are actually honest-to-good-

ness *grateful* to meet a woman who really enjoys oral sex. Some
of the less lucky Sags' may end up with women who grit their
teeth and "put up with his liking for it" -- but they never, never
forget that woman in their past -- the one who put her mouth on
their sex and sucked it tenderly, passonately and loved every
minute of it.

You can run out and buy those books we told you about, but
all you really need to remember are three little points:

*Indulge yourself in oils that smell and taste delicious. Take a
shower together before you make love.*

Use your lips and never your teeth.

Share the fantasy...

You've given your lover the experience of simulating nature.
Now let him indulge his true fantasy which is to make love in
the outdoors, with only a possum or deer admiring from the
sidelines. All you have to do to bring this fantasy to life is to
take him to a lodge in the country. One that has private outdoor
saunas.

Then, in the quiet of night, enter this womb-like retreat that
has a red light (that may require you switching bulbs), and
slowly turn up the heat.

As the temperature rises, you pour water on the hot rocks and
that will create steam. Steam and red lights, in case you didn't
realize it, are a very sexy combination. Oil stroked onto each
other's bodies will quickly fill the warmth with perfume.

Now open the door and reach outside to where you left that
bucket of ice. What fun! You can suck on them, let them drip on
your sizzling bodies, etc. *The etc. is always the best part.* For
instance, insert the cube between your teeth and suck the cold
slowly into your mouth. Keep it there until your mouth and
cheeks are icy cold and then -- put out the fire between his legs.

There is nothing more erotic -- actually the word is excruciat-
ing -- than this steaming sizzzle.

The call of the wild...

For the truly adventurous and sound of heart, now is the time
to climax in the outdoors, under a velvet black sky, with only
the sounds of thunder and lightening rumbling and then later,
much, much later. . .the quiet of the last cricket chirping.

Strangers in Paradise...

Another favorite fantasy is to have sex with a stranger. Now we don't want to encourage Sag to look for love in all the wrong places, so you might want to provide the fantasy.

This can be as simple a scenario as meeting him in a bar and pretending you don't know each other. If you *really* like the game, make sure the bar is in a hotel and take him to a room. If you *really, really* like this game, then buy a wig and turn yourself into that sultry brunette or silky blonde that's hidden inside your psyche.

Then introduce *him* to *them*.

CAPRICORN

DEC 22 – JAN 20

RULING PLANET: SATURN

FEMININE, NEGATIVE, EARTH SIGN

EROTIC DRIVE: TO DISCIPLINE

COLORS: BLACK/BROWN

PASSION FLOWER: NARCISSUS

MAGIC SCENT: CYPRESS

GEMS: GARNET/ONYX/MALACHITE

METAL: LEAD

HERBS:

 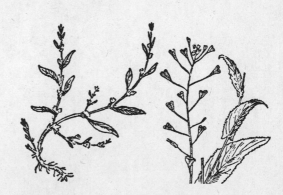

Comfrey   Knot Grass   Shepherd's Purse

"I had to be patient and gentle...I had to make him understand that I could understand everything and accept everything and that he should, too."

Jeanne Moreau, as told to
Marguerite Duras.

Congratulations, you have found the one lover who always "takes care of business" in the bedroom as well as in the boardroom.

Capricorn is an earth sign, ruled by the powerful planet Saturn. Its symbol is the goat, illustrating how tenacious these men can be when going after something they really want. Or someone they truly lust after.

Climbing that mountain, the goat spends much of his time with his eye on the prize, his mind planning and plotting the next move. He won't make that move until he's absolutely positive his footing is on solid ground. This is one lover who doesn't just rush into situations, but uses his tremendous diplomatic skills to get what he wants. With many a Capricorn who doesn't mind being in the spotlight, that goal could be politics or even the acting profession. Wait a minute, there *is* a difference, isn't there?

Your lover's ambitions will always come first, at least in the early part of his life. If he's not married to his career, you can safely consider him hopelessly in love with it. Howard Hughes was a famous Capricorn mover and shaker. So you see, this man can be hungry for power, and his need for control shows up in his personal life as well. Control, discipline, everything in its time and a time for everything. That's Capricorn. It may sound just a *tad* anal retentive, but never forget that Capricorn, with all his outward reserve and dignity, is also a lover who seeks an outlet for his passions. He wants a woman who can see through the reserve, break its shell, and touch the depths of his soul.

However, the search for this mate becomes more difficult

because Capricorn is very demanding. Mainly because he's already judging the kind of wife his public expects. Yes, he is *very* pragmatic; very aware of his image when it comes to choosing social ties that help or hurt his ambitions.

So once your lover is proud to show you off to his business and personal friends, consider yourself halfway to your goal -- which is to, let us *never* forget, seduce this man's heart, mind, body and soul.

WHAT TURNS HIM ON?

Like most men, Capricorn would like to find someone who can play two roles. The main role as the eternal loving woman and wife. But unlike the second role being a version of Madonna (the entertainer *not* the Mother), with Capricorn, the second role needed is Madonna, the *Mother,* not the entertainer.

He keeps it pretty well hidden but your lover needs you to be maternal and supportive while he's struggling up the ladder. He may act as though he can chew nails for breakfast, but actually, he's a lot more sensitive and insecure and he can suffer many bouts of depression.

But make no mistake about it, he will get to the top of that mountain whether it takes a year, ten years or a lifetime. Perhaps that's why those born under the sign of Capricorns can expect to live long lives -- they've been given the time in which to accomplish big dreams.

WHAT TURNS HIM OFF?

This practical earth sign has his feet dug so firmly in the earth that his heels are touching Peking! He's not interested in a woman who might be considered "flighty" or "far out." Remember, he's very concerned with image, mainly his. So if you're intrigued by the metaphysical, (including astrology), be prepared not to have him share your fascination. Of course, you may be lucky enough to find an evolved Capricorn, one who's lived a few lifetimes, and if that's the case, he may know more about astrology than you do. But for the most part, these fellows raise a cynical eyebrow when conversation turns to any-thing they can't see, touch or deposit!

Also, in the same way that a Sagittarius throws ritual to the wind, Capricorn pays it deep homage. Take that a few steps further and you'll understand how important "social rituals" are to him. How important, you ask? Appear for a date wearing a dress that shows your appendix scar and you'll find out. Dare to embarrass him at a business dinner by having one drink too many, or, heavens forbid, play footsie under the table, and that will be the end of the bliss that could have been.

Yes, it's important that you be conservative in public, and save any sexual outrageousness for the bedroom where lusty Capricorn will really appreciate it.

Never forget that under his controlled exterior lies the soul of a true erotic and lustful satyr. Exactly where did you think the expression "horny old goat" came from anyway?

IS CAPRICORN A ONE-WOMAN MAN?

Yes, this is the long-distance runner, the man who respects the vows he took and will do anything (remember his tenacity) to make his marriage work.

Happily for you, this lover is so busy building an empire that his energies -- after satisfying little old insatiable you -- are pretty well spent. So even if he has ideas in his head about fooling around, the rest of him is much too pooped to participate.

But one fact is very important: Capricorn will remain faithful to you as long as you feed his hunger for a full sexual and fantasy life. If he does end up having more than one marriage, it will be because he is frustrated, and still seeking the ideal fulfillment in a sexual union.

DO YOU HAVE WHAT IT TAKES TO SEDUCE CAPRICORN?

In this case, as Olivia just told you, it isn't so much "do you have what it takes to seduce him?" as..."Do you have what it takes to *keep* him?" And that means a strong sexual nature of your own.

This is one lover who seems reserved on the surface (although Capricorn Elvis Presley was the exception to the rule), but all goats seem to be scratching an invisible sexual itch. His passions are strong, and not just for conservative sex play.

Perhaps because he is so reserved and "in control," he yearns to break out -- to experience intense sensations. In short, the sex that Capricorn fantasizes is primitive, passionate and guaranteed to curl your toes.

If you are sure that after the honeymoon, sex in your marriage will be moved to a back burner -- somewhere equal in importance to pet grooming -- then say good-bye to this lover right now. The relationship will never work. Yes, this steadfast man might not divorce you ("what will the boss, neighbors and my aunt Tillie think?") but he has been known to become so depressed if trapped in an unhappy relationship that alcohol has been used as an escape.

Olivia advises that having a few social connections will help your image with this man. And he likes you to be smart, too. All the better to impress his family, boss and good old Aunt Tillie.

WHAT COLOR TURNS HIM ON?

"Ebony is the color of my true love's hair," the poem goes -- and so that is the color for your Capricorn lover. Perhaps it is the endless mystery the color represents (your lover does favor those dark, Germanic philosophers). Or perhaps it is the reserved control of it.

Whatever the reason, black and deep browns are the colors for Capricorn. Come to think of it, when Elvis married Pricilla, didn't he insist on her changing hair color to raven black?

WHAT'S HIS WORST FAULT?

While Scorpio may have his hand in his pocket because he's just happy to see you, a Capricorn lover, you may be sure, is holding onto his loose change. Yes, it's true that this man has a fear of doing without material things later in life (perhaps due to a poor childhood or just his own fears), but the outcome is that he tends to be a wee, tiny bit "tight-fisted." Of course, once you work slowly, relentlessly and *lovingly* on getting him to unwind and be a freer spirit -- you might see some changes in this area, too.

Also, Capricorn can become a bit of a snob. Damn if he doesn't have his eye on the top of that mountain for so long that he's blind to what's really important on the way up. If you see tendencies in this area, get out your garden shears and nip them in the bud. Status will always be important to him, but when it becomes *everything*, and he judges people by whether they have it or not, then he needs a smart lady to help him wise up.

It's also very important that you help him to "lighten up" in other ways, too. His nose being constantly pressed to the grindstone can cause periods of depression that you don't want to know about. In his worst moments, your lover may be tempted to turn to alcohol and you know that's the beginning of a dead-end road.

What do you do when the blues set in? Try to remain your wonderful optimistic self. Show him that instead of thinking the glass is always half empty -- and who the hell took the missing half?? -- it's smarter to consider the glass *half full*. Share your wisdom that his worth is what he *is*, not what he has. It may take a few lifetimes for him to see the light, but you're not in a hurry, are you?

DOES HE HAVE A TEMPER?

There might be times when you'll want to say, "Yell at me, throw something, anything, just don't be so melancholy and depressed!" That's how your lover's anger might implode on itself. At these times he'll become horribly fatalistic and do a lot of moaning about how it was "just meant to be this way, etc. etc."

The best thing to do is to untie the noose around his neck, take the razor from his hand, hide his magnum and talk it all out. Having the very smart, pragmatic mind that he does, Capricorn will soon see the sense of what you're saying and feel a lot better.

IS CAPRICORN GOOD WITH CHILDREN?

There's an old expression: "The parents have tasted of sour grapes and the children's teeth are set on edge." That illustrates how important it is not have our children suffer for our hangups.

So your lover has to remember to "lighten up" with his children, too. He can't keep them in line and disciplined 24 hours a day.

On the positive side, his children will love having him for a father, because they know that he'll always be there for them. To help with the homework, to get them out of jams, to discuss the smartest way they can reach their dreams. Jon Voight is a Capricorn daddy who is well known for being a caring, wonderful parent.

WHAT DOES CAPRICORN CALL HOME?

If you know anything about the psychology of color, than you know that gray represents detachment. It's a fair guess that you'll find this color wall to wall in your lover's apartment. Oh yes, his place will be very expensive looking, after all, Capricorn cares about his perceived status. However, in the same way that so much of our corporate world is bathed in gray (we don't want to get too human on Wall Street, do we??) so might this lover prefer gray that has all the emotional content of granite!

Capricorn will tend to like more formal surroundings, too. If he can afford it, expect to find antiques that give him a taste of the history and solidity he loves. French clocks, Italian chairs, or perhaps even an early American pine hutch. As long as the furniture is traditional, and costs a small fortune, it will appeal to your lover.

Of course, once you are firmly esconced in his life, you can introduce the luxury of casual pillows tossed here and there, a bit of turquoise or fuschia against the grays. Just tread carefully, knowing that your man will need time to loosen up, to relax and not depend on *things* to tell him who he is. He may even become wise enough to realize that no matter how much he pays for something, in the end it's the ultimate ease of life that counts.

Note: Make him think about the word "disease" and what it tells us — that lack of ease in our minds can cause havoc. This peace of mind is the only true luxury we can all possess.

HOW DO YOU DRESS FOR A CAPRICORN?

You know that perfect "little black dress" that has been touted in every social circle since Eve? Well, Capricorn pays it the homage it deserves and then some.

Just take the "idea" of that little black dress and turn it into a sophisticated, stunning, sexy black number with a little skin showing around the shoulders and your man will love it. It's that exciting combination of the proper combined with sexual promise that will have your Capricorn lover hyperventilating.

RECIPE FOR A PERFECT EVENING

The sign of Capricorn is paramount in Yoga (even India is ruled by it) and that illustrates how aware your lover is of the need to exercise. Yoga would be a perfect outlet for Capricorn, letting him control the health of his body and train his mind on the more spiritual aspects of life. If he hasn't yet tried it, suggest that you take lessons together. If he's too inhibited to go to a class, pick up an audio tape of Yoga instruction and you can both do it at home.

Once your man is centered, truly in control of mind and emotions, there's no limit to how far he can go in life.

When it comes to food, too, your lover will understand that it's smarter to eat what's good for him. Although he loves fine restaurants (especially if his expense account is picking up the check), he basically has simple tastes when it comes to food.

His cell salt is Phosphate of Calcium. Since Capricorn rules the knees and bones, Calcium is important in his diet. Give to him in milk, strawberries, blueberries, lettuce and cucumbers, to name a few examples. And when you're cooking for him, make sure he has enough spinach, whole wheat, rye, barley and salt-water fish in his diet.

What herbs are beneficial to Capricorn? Comfrey root, Slippery Elm (it strengthens the bones, which will help Capricorn's weak knees) and Wintergreen. If you like to use Thyme in your cooking, all the better, because it's another Capricorn herb.

Just go easy on dishes you make with garlic and onion. He likes them, he just doesn't want to advertise them. As for the table setting -- make the whole atmosphere cheerful and homey. Flowers and color everywhere.

A bottle of light, rose wine is what to serve with the following:

FIRST STEP: VOLUPTUOUS CHICKEN BREASTS

Skinned chicken breasts
1 stick butter
1 tbs chopped onion
1 cup chopped mushrooms
1 cup whipping cream
1/4 cup sherry
1 tbs wheat flour
2 tbs water
wild rice

Put a stick of butter in a skillet and sauté skinned chicken
breasts until they're lightly browned. Then remove from pan.
Put the onion and fresh mushrooms in the skillet and sauté
them until tender. Add the cup of whipping cream and the sherry. Put the chicken back and cook over low heat for 20 minutes.
Then take out the chicken and add flour and water. Mix well.
Keep stirring till creamy.
   Serve the chicken on a bed of wild rice and garnish with
parsley.

SECOND STEP: PHALLIC STRING BEANS

1 lb fresh string beans
1 tsp olive oil
1/4 cup chopped onion
1/3 cup chopped tomato
1 garlic clove crushed
1 tbs mined parsley
1/2 tsp basil
1/4 tsp thyme
1/4 tsp fennel
1/4 tsp salt
1/8 tsp pepper

Cook the beans in boiling water for about three minutes (they
should remain crisp). Drain and rinse in cold water. In a non-
stick skillet, add the olive oil and sauté onion for two minutes.
Add the tomato, garlic, parsley, all the spices and simmer for
five minutes. Add the string beans, let it sit for five minutes and
then toss.

INTERMISSION:

The music is playing softly in the living room. It's the time to take your lover's hand and ask for the next dance. Capricorn loves to dance and it's the perfect time to hold each other and feel everything that words can't say.

THIRD STEP: TAPIOCA TEASE

4 tart apples, peeled and cored
1/4 cup quick-cooking tapioca
1 1/4 cups boiling water
pinch of sugar
1/4 tsp cinnamon
1/4 tsp nutmeg

Heat your oven at 350 F. Then combine tapioca, water and salt in top of your double boiler and cook until transparent. Put the apples in a greased 12-quart baking dish and fill centers of apples with combined sugar, cinnamon and nutmeg. Pour tapioca over the apples and bake about a half hour until apples are tender.
Ask if he wants coffee or more rosé wine.

WHAT'S THE MOST SENSITIVE PART OF HIS BODY?

Getting this lover to his knees is easy -- simply begin to caress them. Yes, this is the part of the body that has probably given your lover a bit of trouble. It's a rare Capricorn that hasn't suffered some sort of knee injury. In the spiritual sense, Capricorn has got to learn "to bend" and to be flexible.
Be aware though that once you tap the erotic nature of this lover, it will be like a flood. Feelings will pour forth that you must be able to handle. Remember, I told you that the suppressed sexual nature of a Capricorn runs wild once it finds release.
As with the other signs, a full body massage is a wonderful

way to get him to unwind, mentally, emotionally and down to his toes. Don't forget to warm the massage oil in your hands before applying it to his skin. Have you bought the scented candles? Do you have the right soothing music on the stereo?

If you do it right, you'll have to tell him again and again that "It's time to go home." But then again, unlike your lover who sometimes delivers justice instead of mercy, you might let him to stay till morning

WHAT IS THAT ROMANTIC GETAWAY?

Your Capricorn has a great respect for the past and for its ceremonies. Do you know anyone who knows anyone who makes appointments for the Pope? That's too bad. Well, there's still the pageantry of Britain to see. Or, if that's outside your vacation budget, there's always a trip to colonial Williamsburg in Virginia.

If you absolutely can't leave home, then find the oldest, most historic hotel in town and learn all about it. Needless to say, Olivia wants it charming and luxurious besides historic, the last thing you need to do is to make reservations, snuggle up in bed, and find yourself dodging falling plaster.

If it's the right place, you'll find yourself lying in your lover's arms in the best room's four poster bed. Then you begin to fascinate Capricorn with stories of the ancient intrigue and politics that took place in that very spot.

Note from Olympia: If it's just a nice Mom and Pop operation, use your imagination to create wild tales of infamous politicians who wheeled and dealed there; famous actresses who enjoyed secret, torrid affairs on that very same four poster. It will definitely be a turn on for Capricorn to have sex with you in the middle of all that historic intrigue.

"The wonderful thing about old hotels is that they made the walls very thick," you murmur as you slip into his arms.

"That's fine...as long as I can hear you," he whispers back. "I want to hear every cry, every moan you make."

You smile in the darkness, because you know that no matter how long it takes...your tenacious Capricorn lover *always* gets what he wants.

HOW TO PLEASE CAPRICORN SEXUALLY.

When the time comes that you and your lover are intimate

and pretty much trust each other...then it's time to invite him to *a little surprise party*. That's right, a little surprise party, and that's exactly how you say it. When he asks who or what, tell him nothing, only when. Then when he comes to the door at the appointed time, and you know this man is always right on time, greet him in your most outrageously sexy penoir, night-gown, teddy, bikini, or just plain skin -- whatever makes you feel totally female and seductive. Then tell him that yes, the surprise party is on, and the surprise is that it's *just* the two of you.

Before I get to party time, let's talk a little bit about what you've learned about this man. In bed, of course. You know he likes to take control, that he may show passion far easier than other deeper held emotions. That he likes anal sex. Oh, he hasn't told you that yet?? Well, an affair is full of surprises, isn't it?

Anyway, you may know a lot about him, but what you may not know is that he fears losing the very control he wants over others. And yet, at the same time, he's fascinated by the thought of it. Actually, he wants to lose control, to turn himself over to a lover's desires...he thinks about it, fantasizes it...now he's going to finally get it.

Take him in hand...

The moment he enters the room, you must take control. The forces you're going to fight are his prim and proper anal reten-tive thoughts. Believe me, that's one worthy opponent!

The first tactic is for you to separate him from the day person he is -- that fellow with the impeccable suit and polished every-thing.

First things first: get him out of that suit. Begin with the shoes. Having him remove his shoes is a very strange sensation to someone like Capricorn who is probably even used to walk-ing on white carpets with leather shoes. It's always disarming and his senses are now telling him...play or run.

If he chooses to play, *you* remove his socks.

Now, telling him about the surprise party, start turning off lamps, slowly, slowly, and lighting candles. As you walk around the room, setting the stage, bend over from the waist as often as possible. Is the music right? Have you handed him a glass of wine or whatever aphrodisiac turns him on?

If you've never undressed a man, remember two things: do it very slowly and try not to take your eyes from his. The best

thing to first remove from a Capricorn lover is his jewelry. Strip
him of that status, image-making armor and he'll feel immediately vulnerable.

Whatever you do, don't get all passionate here and rip the
clothes from the poor man's body. He'll panic and you'll wind
up owing him a fortune for a shredded Italian shirt. Slowly, ever
so slowly, unbutton that shirt, but -- as you draw the sleeves
down to his wrists -- stop there. Let the shirt hang from his
wrists. This is his first taste of losing control, of bondage.

If you have natural talent for this sort of thing, you should be
able to remove his belt in one flick of the wrist. However, on
second thought, he may consider you a professional, so take
whatever time you need. Now we're at the most delicious part.

Again, we're in no hurry. . .the only time you should whisk
down a man's zipper is in a drive-in movie or under a bridge in
Central Park.

Note: Hang on to the belt.

Have your Capricorn lover stand and hold onto the back of a
chair while you slide his pants down his legs. At this point,
pause and check out his corporate image. If it isn't hard in
anticipation, then tell him to go home and think about it for a
week.

All others may happily proceed to the next step: take off his
trousers. Then, remembering that in a proper seduction, nothing
on a man should ever be yanked, including his underwear. Take
them off, too.

Tell him not to remove his hands from the chair or he'll be
punished. If he doesn't respond, then he's still in his corporate
mode. If he's not willing to separate the man from the boy -- a*nd
you've got to make him do this or he'll never really let loose* --
then the game has to be called on account of panic.

If he challenges you at this point, saying that he doesn't
believe you'll do it, and you can hear in his tone that he's willing, give him a brief but spicy taste of leather. Tell him to keep
his hands firmly on the chair. As a matter of fact, tell him to
bend over. When he does, instruct him to spread his legs. That
gives him more sense of your control, and it's a very sexy feeling for him.

Picture this, you now have your Capricorn lover totally naked
in your living room, dining room or foyer. The lights are dim,
the music is wonderful and his hard on could cut through red-
wood. Most wonderful is that perhaps for the first time in his
sexual life -- he is being controlled. This man who does just

about everything according to schedule, now doesn't know what to expect. He is a boy again and everything is possible.

You have many fascinating options now. You may lift up his shirt, kneel down and put your lips on his most vulnerable self ...or you can take him into the bedroom where he will sit on the bed. Stand before him and bring his face close to your own hot body...then blindfold him.

Share the fantasy...

Capricorn's fantasy is the same as the one above, only the location is different.

In this scenario, you visit him in his office, close the door, and begin to take off his clothes. Pause only long enough to allow him to reach for the phone and tell his secretary to hold all calls.

Now if your man shares his work space with a few other dozen people, it may present a problem. Happily, you can always come late and work overtime.

AQUARIUS

JAN 21 – FEB 19

RULING PLANET: URANUS

MASCULINE, POSITIVE, AIR SIGN

EROTIC DRIVE: TO EXPERIMENT

COLOR: WHITE

PASSION FLOWER: PANSY

MAGIC SCENT: ACACIA

GEM: AMETHYST

METAL: LEAD

HERBS:

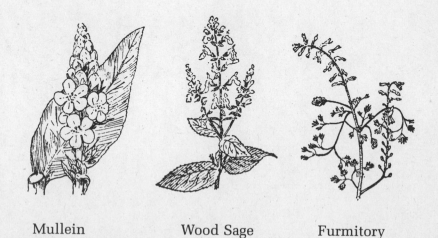

Mullein   Wood Sage   Furmitory

"When I think of sex, I think of it as a domain only partially explored, the greater part, for me at least, remains mysterious and unknown...possibly forever unknown."

Henry Miller

Some men walk to the beat of a different drummer, and Aquarius, the air sign ruled by the planet Uranus, illustrates how exciting that rhythm can be. The symbol for Aquarius is the Waterbearer. Many people are confused by this because, after all, it is an air sign, isn't it? Yes, but the Waterbearer symbolizes your lover's need to dispense knowledge, pouring it from the river of life to humanity. If it all sounds a little ambitious for the average man, never forget that your lover is *anything but* average. He wants to change the world, and unlike most of us who grow up and trade in our dreams for fat corporate perks, Aquarius remains eternally idealistic.

That isn't to say that he will ever have the chances in life to change the world for the better, but in his way, he will never stop dreaming the impossible dream.

That's why it's been said that your lover is detached, relating better to people as a group than as individuals. Unlike a Capricorn who is very concerned with his image, Aquarius could care less. Take me as I am, or not at all, is the unsaid, and you'll hear it loud and clear.

Your lover is progressive, and his planet Uranus, able to change the world by sudden upheaval, makes him almost impossible to "figure". He is the reformer. The one who exchanges the old for the new. His actions can be electric (this sign actually rules electricity) and when the dust settles, life will never be the same. It may be radically different, even stranger than fiction, but chances are your world will be better for it.

If you've never experienced the sexual bliss of having your

mind and body totally consumed at the same time -- then your
Aquarian love affair will open doors to an incredible new
world. You see, just physical sex isn't what this man is all
about. He wants total emotional and spiritual involvement --
and he wants it yesterday!

I've said that sexual nirvana is what Aquarius *wants* -- I'm
not promising that he's smart enough, talented enough or spiritually evolved enough to guarantee this bliss...but you're both
going to collect intense memories trying to attain it.

So cancel all appointments for the next year or two. You've
got a lot of experimentation ahead of you with the great sexual
experimenter of the zodiac...you lucky, lucky girl.

WHAT TURNS HIM ON?

Like Don Quixote, who dreamed the impossible dream, your
Aquarius has visions that few can see; ideals that most have for-
saken and forgotten. If you're a "meat and potatoes thinker,"
then your poor lover is going to starve to death. He's an intellectual whose mind must be turned on before his body can feel the
first quake.

By the way, when I use the word "intellectual", that doesn't
necessarily mean that your mate is schooled in the conventional
sense. He may even be a kindergarten drop out, or not know
which spoon to use at your sister's wedding. It doesn't matter,
because his intellect is constantly searching for knowledge.
Besides, nothing is more charismatic in a man than a blending
of street and book smarts. Some of the most intriguing males in
history have been self-educated. If you want a fascinating example, just look at "Aquarius born" Abraham Lincoln.

Now let's rub the Vaseline off our magnifying glass (that's
what they used to use on their camera lenses in Hollywood
when filming anyone over 12!) and let's take a good look at you.

Do you work for any causes? Is your altruism a little rusty
around the edges? Do you consider yourself a humanitarian?
Oh, you have been known to say that charity begins at home???
Aquarius is his brother's keeper and, sister, the best way to
seduce this lover heart, mind, body and soul is to think as much
about others as yourself.

Paul Newman is a good example of a contemporary Aquarius
who marches to the beat of his own drummer. From the summer
camp he created for terminally ill kids to his involvement in

politics, he's not content to be just an incredibly handsome face and also one of our great actors -- oh no, this Aquarius is always trying to make the world a better place.

WHAT TURNS HIM OFF?

Remember the lady named Ivy because, she only knew how to cling? Well, she'd better not try her luck with this lover. Aquarius must feel free. He wants a companion, but definitely not one who will make him feel bound by rules and laws. It's a rare Aquarius who enters into marriage without icy cold feet....and it's a wise woman who knows it's impossible to harness the wind.

Let your lover know that you only want to be his partner and spiritual companion, not the warden who is about to rob him of his freedom. That means that if he wants to take a few days off and head into the desert all by his lonesome, don't sulk. Don't threaten. Don't become so insecure that you're paranoid it's all about your flunking your diet. Aquarius just needs space, literally, in which to collect his thoughts and feel centered again. Trust me, it isn't another woman's touch Aquarius seeks, only the chance to get in touch with himself.

It's also important that you stick to whatever promises you make your lover. A person's word is sacred to Aquarius and once it's broken, so is the relationship.

IS AQUARIUS A ONE-WOMAN MAN?

Yes, you can relax in knowing that if you should marry your Aquarius, he won't be spending his energies and time somewhere else.

It's true that many of this sign spend their youth escaping matrimony, but when they finally get around to it, it's for better or for worse until death does you part. He may not always show his love and devotion the way you'd like -- this man has a frustrating detachment -- but he'll be there for you and only you when it counts.

DO YOU HAVE WHAT IT TAKES TO
SEDUCE AQUARIUS?

It's time for a truth test. Are you really the non-conformist your Aquarius lover wants, or are you the girl who is secretly terrified of those romantic rebels who shout, "Rules were made to be broken!"

Your lover is this rebel at heart, and unless you have what it takes to buck the system with him (whether on a large political scale or in his frat club), or at least give him roaring support, you might be too tame to keep his interest.

Next question: In your personal life, are you open to new thinking? Aquarius has read scores of books about metaphysics. Mention the word *occult* and watch his eyes light up. The strange and unknown doesn't scare him, they fascinate him. Do you have this kind of relentless curiosity, or do you find tradition as comforting as your flannel nightgown?

Be prepared for many hours spent playing the "what if?" game. The subject may be philosophy, religion or the color of your hair...but he'll always wonder "what if things were different?" Never forget this man has the sense of adventure to actually find out how different life can be -- by living it. Fate or finances may never give him the chance to explore the world (and his fascinating psyche) the way he'd like...but he'll always be dreaming of that "what if"!

Note: It's usually around the time when Aquarius gets gutsy enough to add "Why not?" to "What if?" that he starts to rock the boat.

WHAT COLOR TURNS HIM ON?

Silver is the color for this sign and that shimmering, electric silvery blue. Of course you can wear silver in everything from blouses to nightgowns. You remember nightgowns...that overpriced article of clothing that looks so delightful and sexy on your body for about five minutes before it slides to the bottom of the bed?

Don't forget silvery-blue eye shadow. It will probably stay on longer than that nightgown!

WHAT'S HIS WORST FAULT?

Stubbornness is a trait of which many Aquarians are guilty --
especially when they're trying to convince you of something.
You can show them the body, the murder weapon and the coro-
ner's report -- and they'll *still* stick to their suicide theory. At its
worst, this trait can turn into bullying. But stick to your guns; if
you're right, in the end Aquarius will only admire you more for
it. Of course, if you're wrong...have you contemplated the clois-
tered life? How do you look in black with white around the collar line?

Another less than attractive trait is being absent-minded. That
is hardly a crime worth reporting, but try to remember that
when your lover has you wandering around with him at two in
the morning trying to remember where he parked the car. The
fellow who first tied a red balloon to his car antenna after he
parked it, was probably Aquarius.

DOES AQUARIUS HAVE A TEMPER?

He definitely is not a screamer or tantrum thrower. If anything, you have to work hard to get Aquarius to know that you
exist. He's so busy living in that fascinating mind of his that
mere mortals are often an annoyance.

Of course, once you're his lover, then you *definitely* have his
attention. He may get stubborn in an argument, he may even
imitate your worst traits, you know, the way you tend to stutter
when angry or pull at that lock of hair when nervous (Aquarius
has a talent for this below the belt tactic) but you'll very rarely
hear him raise his voice.

To be perfectly honest though, there is a less evolved type
that has been known to have an explosive temper. (These people are suspected of not playing with a full deck by the more
staid players in the zodiac). It's usually when they feel restrict-
ed by some archaic rule. They know they're right, and why the
hell are people so dumb, why do they live in the past, why does
the new always frighten them, why won't someone listen???
The frustration builds up and before you know it...isn't that
Aquarius on a soap box over there in the park?

IS AQUARIUS GOOD WITH CHILDREN?

This is one sign that actually doesn't suffer from the "empty nest syndrome." They want their children to be independent and when they finally take wing, papa is very proud indeed.

You can expect your lover to fill your children's minds with thought-provoking ideas. He'll want them to go to the most progressive schools and when the eight year old comes home and reports that he led a march against the tyranny of the principal... guess who's going to be beaming with pride?

But it will be up to you, mama, to give old-fashioned discipline when it's needed. Your man will be a great friend to the kids, but parental control including curfews and limits will probably have to come from you.

WHAT DOES AQUARIUS CALL HOME?

The moment you step into your lover's nest, you'll be able to see that the surroundings are as unique as he is. What is it, you wonder? It's not the furniture, everything looks moderately priced and not that unusual. It's not the simple charcoals on the wall, or the pieces of American Indian pottery. What, you ask yourself, gives your lover's home such a special feeling.

Well, unlike Capricorn who feels more secure with costly furniture, or Taurus who prefers his home opulent, or Leo who wants it to be an Architectural Digest showplace, your man doesn't care about the cost of things, only their effect on his psyche.

Nothing will be fussy; not a lot of furniture or dust catchers on shelves. There may be much glass and low couches that are arranged so as to make conversation easy. Colors will be muted and relaxing.

Also, there isn't any object placed "just so" for effect. No book is open to a page calculated to impress. What you see is what you get this home seems to say -- because the effect that Aquarius most cares about is one of simplicity and comfort.

In short, it will be a place in which to unwind and forget the whole busy, silly, ulcer-making civilization outside...and that's exactly what Aquarians think of as home.

HOW DO YOU DRESS FOR AQUARIUS?

You don't have to worry about what's proper or "politically correct." Your lover doesn't mind if you break all the rules and wear your bomber jacket to the opera. A fake tattoo when you meet his relatives? Adorable! Your Aquarius will probably think all your more zany ideas are delightfully shocking because he loves to shock. As a matter of fact, the more eyebrows he can raise in an evening, the more entertaining.

Also, rather than wanting to see you lead a society fashion parade, or impress snobs he refuses to walk five feet out of his way for, your lover just wants you to be comfortable...in comfortable shoes...in comfortable thinking...and to hell with the critics!

RECIPE FOR A PERFECT EVENING

In case yours is a brand-new affair with Aquarius, check to see if he's a vegetarian. Many of his sign are, or semi-vegetarians and eat only chicken or fish. Then too, your lover might be all the way "out there" and feed only on a macrobiotic diet. You see, if this new-age man thinks a certain diet can benefit him spiritually or psychically, he'll be tempted to adopt it.

Try to and make the dinner as casual as possible. A lot of Grandma's crystal and complicated flaming dishes that would delight Leo, will prove to have the opposite effect on this paragon of simplicity.

His cell salt is Sodium Chloride and he likes the taste of salt (its function being to provoke thirst, which in turn guarantees a plentiful water supply throughout his body) so use it when cooking, but also be sure to feed him foods that are high in its content: spinach, apples, figs, cucumbers, strawberries, chestnuts , asparagus, radishes, carrots, etc.

Herbs in your lover's diet are very important. If you've ever seen him bent over with leg cramps, then you'll be anxious to try Snake Root. Sounds a little scary? Well, most things do sound scary before we get to know them, and besides, you had better start thinking like an experiment-loving Aquarius. Now read the words "Snake Root" again and immediately say out loud, "How foreign, how strange, how exciting, I can't wait to try it." Now say it again without clutching your throat!

Actually, this herb is known as a remedy for the very painful leg cramps that plague Aquarians. Just ask the specialist in the herb department to educate you on how much to put in foods, or in teas, etc.

Don't forget to serve up some interesting dinner companions, as well. Aquarius, who loves groups, will be delighted to dine in unusual company. Remember that friend who had the out-of-the body experience? Well, if she's back in it, invite her over. Oh yes, remember that college buddy with the fascinating conspiracy theory about the media controlling the vote? Invite him over, too. Aquarius loves provocative conversation that manages to spark his mind and his appetite.

Note: Just because your lover is a man of relatively simple tastes, doesn't mean you should forget the music or the candles, or anything else that will stir his erotic juices.

FIRST STEP: ENTICING BISQUE

1 package of frozen chopped broccoli (10 oz.)
1 small onion diced
1/8 tsp ground pepper
Dash of salt
1 cup water
2 cups skim milk
1 whole clove garlic
1 tbs cornstarch

Place the broccoli, onion, clove of garlic and pepper and water in a saucepan. Cover and cook the broccoli until it is very soft. Remove the garlic. Process the broccoli and the liquid in electric blender, then return to saucepan. Combine the skim milk and the cornstarch into a smooth paste, stir it in the broccoli mixture, Heat, stirring constantly until the bisque has slightly thickened.

SECOND STEP: ORGASMIC SALAD

1 head of spinach thoroughly washed
2 hard boiled eggs (yolks removed), chopped
1/2 tsp garlic powder

Dash of pepper
3 1/2 tbs tarragon vinegar
1 tbs water

Arrange the spinach leaves artistically on a plate. Sprinkle them with the cooked egg white and then stir together the garlic powder, pepper, vinegar and water. Pour this dressing over the salad and serve.

Note: If you want to make this dressing in advance, keep it separate from the spinach leaves until ready to serve so that the salad will remain crisp.

THIRD STEP: FELLATIO FETTUCCINE

1/2 cup (1 stick) butter
8 oz fresh or frozen Alaskan King crabmeat.
3/4 cup whipping cream
1/2 cup grated Parmesan cheese
1/2 tsp coarsely ground pepper
Dash of salt
12 ounces fettuccine cooked and drained
2 tbs fresh parsley, chopped
1 clove garlic, minced

Melt the butter in heavy skillet over medium heat. Add the garlic and sauté until golden brown. Stir in the crabmeat, cream, Parmesan, pepper and salt and stir until well blended. Pour the crab sauce over fettuccine in a large serving bowl and toss well. Sprinkle with parsley.

INTERMISSION:

Leave your lover to the company of your fascinating guests and put on the gourmet coffee blend. Then take the following scrumptious dessert out of the refrigerator.

FOURTH STEP: SENSUAL STRAWBERRIES

1 quart strawberries
1 1/2 tsp lemon juice
3 tbs sugar
2 cups heavy cream
1/2 cups confectioner's sugar

Wash the strawberries very well, then crush and strain them. Mix with sugar and lemon juice. Whip cream until stiff, adding the sugar slowly, and blend with strawberries. Place in a quart mold and freeze. Cut into 5 to 8 sinful portions.

WHAT'S THE MOST SENSITIVE PART OF HIS BODY?

You'll have great adventures with Aquarius, but, unfortunately, one of them will not be climbing the Himalayas. Your lover can suffer from vertigo, an inner-ear imbalance that pains many people born in this sign. Figuratively speaking, the very nearness of you may throw this man off balance, but since Aquarius rules the ankles, his physical balance in the real world might be off, too.

A massage can release the tension that causes headaches and thwarts any leg cramps that might be building up.

WHERE IS THAT ROMANTIC GETAWAY?

Aquarius loves a landscape that looks untouched by man...rugged, complete in its own primitive beauty. Someplace where he can feel totally free. One of his favorite haunts is the barren beauty of the desert.

A week or a month or a lifetime in the Southwest will be just what this fantasy demands. Start in the red rock splendor of Sedona, Arizona. If you haven't already been to this magnificent spot, you're in for a treat. This beautiful landscape offers even more than being incredibly sensuous -- it's thought to be one of the power centers of the world. Seekers of truth come here from all over the globe to meditate.

What better place to give your man a long-planned, unique

sexual experience that touches both your souls?

With the intense sun above, you and your Aquarius will be shaded by the rocky landscape. The magic in the earth is a magnet...drawing you both closer to it, until you are merged as one body.

High above you a crow is a black dot in the silvery blue sky, and you think about Carlos Castenada's books on magic in the Southwest desert. What omen did it mean when a black crow was sighted? You try to remember...but your lover's impatient hands are wiping every thought from your mind...and then the wind dies down until you can feel only his warm breath on your cheek...and then...

HOW TO PLEASE AQUARIUS SEXUALLY.

Remember I mentioned that Aquarius loves to experiment? There is not a better guide to erotic experimentation than the famed Kama Sutra.

In the candle-lit intimacy of your bedroom -- or whatever room is most appealing -- put on the hypnotic music of an Indian flute and place pillows and body oil beside you. Oh yes, make sure that your favorite perfume or oil is among them.

Just in case you have led a sheltered life and actually don't know about the Kama Sutra, let me tell you that it is a book guiding you through a host of sexual positions -- one more erotic leading to the next. It can be bought in book stores dealing in metaphysical subjects. For generations, lovers have looked through its pages together, then practiced positions that brought them closer in the most spiritual sense.

What you want to do is get Aquarius to sit in a full lotus position if he can attain it, and half if he can't. There are many picture in the book illustrating the best way to sit in lotus. You will also see that this is the position assumed for the first sexual union in the Kama Sutra.

Note: Olivia must share some tantalizing information with you. The thought of perversion turns your lover on, and watching you in a mirror -- while the candles flicker and cast eerie shadows -- will give him the feeling of the forbidden.

It's time to take the oil, rub it slowly over your breasts as he watches...slowly down your stomach and between your legs. Then bend over and work the oil up from the tips of your toes, up your calves and up your thighs.

Then take your oiled hand and caress his sex until it's straining for you.

Now this is the part that separates the girls from the females who truly understand erotica. Take the perfume and put just a few drops on your fingers and draw your hand slowly up between your legs. Then straddle him with that scent of perfume close to his face, and with your two hands lightly on his shoulders, silently lower your body onto his chest, lightly brushing the most sensitive part of you as you slip down his muscular stomach.

As you feel his heat ready to enter you, take ever so long sliding down the shaft. Now with your legs wrapped around him you are in the famous shared lotus position

Take your time and savor the moment, not necessarily the movement. The idea in this position is to feel him inside you and to join physically and spiritually. The moment is one of meditation, as you use your internal muscles to squeeze the love between you.

It takes many sessions of practice to get it right, and this thought should have you cancelling all Tupperware party invitations. If you are a really serious student, you may one day enjoy the expertise graduation brings…when you will be able to draw the sexual energy up your spine to the base of your brain, where at the point of orgasm, your body explodes and your mind sees stars.

Note: Olivia advises you do only one position a night and practice it until you can't tell where he begins and you end.

That is true nirvana.

Share the fantasy…

You lover also likes the latest gadgets and we are not talking about blenders in the kitchen. This man has a hunger for anything (and anyone) who can awaken sensations in him that he only suspects exist.

Things that go buzz in the night…

Now this necessitates a shopping excursion for you that perhaps you never, in your wildest dreams, thought you would take. Our destination is one of those intriguing shops that sell black leather, silver-studded collars, vibrators that reach your soul, electric Ben wah balls, plus a little item that will be first on your list...the double dildo.

Although you might not have yet entered one of those fascinating shops, I assume that you do know what a dildo is. If not, put this book back on the shelf immediately and never mention it to anyone!

You can tell your Aquarius what you have and let him orchestrate its use, or do it all yourself. Happily, you won't need a degree in advanced engineering to figure out how to give both of you the most pleasure. The use of the double dildo is fairly evident. But suffice it to say that both phalluses can be used at the same time.

Positions are optional. Pleasure is optimum.

PISCES

FEB 20 – MAR 20

RULING PLANET: NEPTUNE

FEMININE, NEGATIVE, WATER SIGN

EROTIC DRIVE: TO UNITE

CARNAL COLOR: VIOLET

PASSION FLOWER: IRIS

MAGIC SCENT: MAGNOLIA

GEM: AQUAMARINE

METAL: PEWTER

HERBS:

 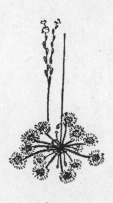 

Bog Bean   Sun Dew   Yarrow

*"I have too many fantasies to
be a housewife...I guess I am
a fantasy."*
Marilyn Monroe

Here is the true romantic of the zodiac. The lover constantly
striving for a magic relationship -- one filled with poetry
and moonlight, tenderness and the emotional crescendos of a
Chopin sonata (who happened to be a Pisces, of course).

Your lover is a water sign, symbolized by two fish that are
seemingly swimming in opposite directions (more on that later),
and ruled by the enigmatic planet Neptune. Thanks to Neptune,
your lover has an elusive, mystical quality. He seems to be seeing something just beyond your vision, listening to creative
muses that he seeks the courage to follow.

Pisces, you will be pleased to know, is open about his desire
for a good relationship. He needs it to grow and to achieve his
dreams. And, make no mistake about it, this complex lover of
yours is a dreamer -- spinning fantasies that might one day be a
reality. Albert Einstein illustrates the heights of genius Pisces
can reach -- all he needs is your support, faith and ability to
dream with him. Of course, a sudden inheritance of about five
million or so from some unknown benefactor wouldn't hurt at all.

WHAT TURNS HIM ON?

As Gerald O'Hara in "Gone With The Wind" told his beautiful
daughter: "Scarlett, always remember that like marries like." So
a Pisces man is attracted to a woman with equal sensitivity; one
who is tuned into a more subtle dimension.

Sometimes it seems that he knows just what you're thinking,
doesn't it? It's almost uncanny. If he says that you really should-
n't take that particular flight, and he doesn't know why, it's just
this *funny* feeling he has -- unpack and immediately call for a

refund. It's not unusual for Pisces to have psychic ability. More psychics are born under this sign than any other. It's this extra sensitivity that makes your lover an outstanding erotic partner in bed -- he is *never* one dimensional.

So many men of this sign sacrifice what they really want in life in order to support the wishes of those they love. While it's wonderful that you've found such a giving, altruistic lover, if he's not careful he's apt to lose his own self along the way.

As a matter of fact, some of your man's self-sacrificing and forgiving nature might be explained by his symbol. Remember those fish? They are also the symbol of Christianity.

Your faith in him is a great turn on. Emotionally and sexually. If your Pisces has a dream that he has yet to realize, show him that you'll work together to make it a reality. Believe in him, because it's a rare Pisces that has the built-in self-confidence to achieve his dreams alone. With your love and faith, however, this man, who is used to swimming upstream to conquer problems, can be capable of tremendous triumphs.

Think about it -- there isn't a better gift to give a lover than faith in him -- it costs you nothing, it doesn't need any gift wrapping, one size fits all, and it will last a lifetime.

WHAT TURNS HIM OFF?

Most Pisces men are never stock market moguls or industry tycoons. Money and power are not their "raison d'être" in life, and so, if it's really important that your mate has a fat income along with a Swiss bank account, this dreamer may not be for you.

I'm definitely not saying that Pisces can't become wealthy, but he doesn't like the mercenary rules of the concrete jungle (where you have to play dirty if you want to be *filthy* rich!) So chances are, he's found a saner niche for himself. Therefore, a very materialistic female, one who, when introduced, takes out her computer and asks "So, exactly what do you drive?" It would be a definite turn off.

Of course, many a Pisces has realized his dream and made a lot of money along the way, but I'll wager that the dreams came first and the reward was just icing on the cake.

IS PISCES A ONE-WOMAN MAN?

Yes, your lover is faithful in the best idealistic, romantic sense of the word. He married you because you were the epitome of his dreams. His only thought was to love, protect and cherish you.

Now that's a big responsibility, isn't it? So, take good care of this gentle, sensitive man. As long as you help keep the romance alive, Pisces will feel towards you the same way he did when you met.

DO YOU HAVE WHAT IT TAKES TO SEDUCE PISCES?

Like the other two water signs, Cancer and Scorpio, your Pisces lover can (figuratively speaking) drown in his emotions. They react to dramas intensely, and it takes a well-balanced partner to ride these tides with him.

That's why a woman with two feet on the ground and the ability to be objective -- to take a few steps away from the problem and then discuss it calmly with her lover -- is the right kind of cool partner.

Remember, too, that Pisces needs to be alone from time to time to simply recharge his batteries. Are you the type who has to be surgically removed from her lover when he wants to go to the bathroom? Don't resent the fact that your man has to be by himself every now and then. This kind of absence will only make his heart grow fonder.

Just between the two of us though, how tactful are you? Your Pisces is a very sensitive creature and if you don't usually think before you speak, he may bleed quietly and not say a word for the rest of the night. Like Cancer, he'll retreat inside his shell to lick his wounds in private. So, if what's on your mind is usually on your tongue -- remember Olivia's warning -- you're going to love spending New Year's recaulking your bathroom tiles!

WHAT COLOR TURNS HIM ON?

Lavender, violet, purple...all these magical hues. Elizabeth Taylor's eyes would be a definite romantic ideal for Pisces (in fact, this very romantic lady happens to be a Pisces). But since we can't all have violet eyes without contact lenses, try wearing these colors to please his desire for the magical.

WHAT'S HIS WORST FAULT?

Well, it's not really his worst fault, and to tell the truth, being as much in love with Pisces as you are, you'll probably be ecstatic he has it.

I'm talking about his ability to put you on a ten foot high pedestal.

He sees you only in your best light. He adores you, he worships you, he thinks you're nothing like your mother?? Watch out! The noise of an idol crashing ten feet to the ground can be deafening. Pisces sets himself up to be disappointed by letting Neptune cloud his vision; seeing only the perfect illusion in place of reality.

Perhaps this sign, more than others, has to be very careful not to run off to the preacher when he feels the heady rush of passion. He doesn't just fall in love with you, he consumes your mind and body, immerses himself in your soul. No, there is no doubt about it, a Pisces male is ready to place himself on the altar of love and let the gods do with him what they may.

So be practical for the both of you. Wait awhile and see if you two are still blissfully happy three months from now. In that way you'll know that Pisces really married the real honest-to-goodness you. Not some fantasy his imagination created. He'll know it too after he survives that traumatic moment when you say: "Sweetheart, don't get scared but this is me in the morning without my make-up, those dumb violet contacts, in a lousy mood, and what the hell's wrong with my mother??"

DOES HE HAVE A TEMPER?

When the average Pisces lover gets angry he finds it really hard to communicate his feelings. That's why I told you that he needs a woman just as sensitive, but not as highly emotional. One who can "talk things out" and give him some perspective on the problem. Many a Pisces, deprived of this outlet, has been known to turn to drink or drugs in a frantic escape.

To make matters more complicated, your Pisces has an extraordinary imagination. Was he *slightly* offended by something you said? Well, by the time he brushes his teeth for bed, his imagination will have blown that mole hill into Mt. McKinley.

Sensitivity and imagination are two qualities that account for many a Pisces entering the acting profession. It's here they can escape reality and act out their vivid fantasies -- while making wonderfully immoral amounts of money.

IS PISCES GOOD WITH CHILDREN?

You can look forward to your man being a perfect companion to your children. He might go a little easy on the disciplining but he'll be right there to encourage them in their ambitions, to share their hurts and their joys.

The nice thing about a Pisces daddy is that he has the imagination to travel with the kids to make-believe place... together they can dream and wander and play and leave the dull old world behind.

WHAT DOES PISCES CALL HOME?

It looks lived in. But somehow the disarray only adds to its charm. It has a soft, romantic feeling. There will probably be lots of plants, lush carpets, lovely pictures and ornaments. Your lover finds it hard to throw away something that reminds him of a particularly happy moment.

Pisces also prefers low, soothing lighting -- so that everything is blended, harmonious -- even when you're together, snuggled on the couch, make sure that your voice is no louder than the night.

HOW DO YOU DRESS FOR PISCES?

If asked, a Pisces would probably confess to wanting to live at the turn of the century: when there was the glow of gaslight, horses on cobblestone roads, and women showed just enough skin to spark the imagination.

So dress for your gentle, romantic Pisces with more skirts than pants. More soft textures than leather. More violets and pastels than crayon colors.

And, of course, use the color lavender whenever and wherever you can.

RECIPE FOR A PERFECT EVENING

It won't surprise you to discover that your water-sign lover finds a seafood menu irresistible. He enjoys exotic, colorful fish dishes with rich sauces and they're even more appreciated when served with his favorite wine.

The cell salt for Pisces is Phosphate of Iron. He needs iron in his diet to keep colds and pulmonary diseases away, so here are a few items to stock up on in your pantry and refrigerator: Spinach (its most potent raw so use it in salads), cabbage, strawberries, onions, raisins, kale, barley, lettuce, radishes, horseradish etc.

As for herbs, there is one that's known for curing every complaint Pisces can imagine -- Irish Moss. It may sound quite foreign and exotic, but check out how to use it at your local health food store. Mothers have been known to add it to soup, where it stays unnoticed by finicky children.

Note: Being a water sign, Pisces is very good at soaking up other peoples vibes, which can be wonderful, or turn into a dining disaster. So if you're planning to invite company for dinner, be very careful it isn't that slightly manic depressive cousin who still isn't over her divorce after seventeen years.

FIRST STEP:

Since Pisces likes a full meal, and will appreciate all the steps along the way, greet him with some tasty hors d'oeuvres. Something simple like nut butter on celery, or whatever your imagination can conjure. Serve a dry white wine.

SECOND STEP:

You can go into the gourmet soup section of your supermarket and pick up a rich, delicious broth...or if you want to prove your undying love for this man...

OYSTER BISQUE TEMPTATION

1 quart oysters, drained (reserve liquid)
1/4 cup butter

1 cup light cream
dash salt
dash pepper
1 clove minced garlic
1/2 thinly sliced onion

Chop the oysters very finely and put them through your food
processor with half of the oyster liquid. Saute onion and garlic
in butter until golden and soft. Then stir in the oyster mixture.
Stir in the remaining ingredients, heat thoroughly, but be careful
not to let it boil. Season to taste with salt and pepper.
NOTE: Serve with crackers.

COQUILLES A L'AMOUR

There's enough food in this recipe to feed 8 people, just in
case you decide to share this memorable evening.

2 pounds scallops
3 chopped carrots, peeled
1 tbs minced onion
1 tbs minced celery
2 cups white wine
1/4 tsp paprika
1/4 cup butter
1/2 pound sliced mushrooms
1/4 cup whole wheat flour
1/4 cup heavy cream
1/2 cup grated Swiss cheese
1/2 cup minced parsley
garlic salt to taste

Place the scallops in a saucepan and add parsley, carrots,
wine and seasonings. Simmer for about 10 minutes and then
remove scallops. Dice scallops, drain the liquid and reserve.
Saute the onion, celery and mushrooms in butter until the
onion is soft. Add reserved liquid.
Combine flour and cream to a smooth paste, then slowly add
to onion mixture. Keep stirring constantly over a low heat until
smooth and thickened. Add scallops; stir. Pile mixture into 8
scallop shells and sprinkle with cheese. Then stick them under

the broiler until they're a delicate golden brown.

INTERMISSION:

By this time, Pisces is thoroughly enchanted with you. You
have managed to serve him wholesome, delicious food and your
friends are charming, intelligent and a great reflection of you. (If
this is too much to expect even of a magician like yourself, you
can always skip the company and have enough food for thirds.)

FOURTH STEP:

There's been much rich food and your Pisces lover might
enjoy a dessert of simple cheese and fruit. Serve it with your
best home made brew.

WHAT'S THE MOST SENSITIVE PART OF HIS BODY?

Pisces rules the feet, and as everyone today knows, reflexology (the art of foot massage) is one the most erotic practices
around. Every part of the foot corresponds to a different part of
the body. While the foot is being massaged, so is the pancreas,
liver, heart and so on. Is your imagination already running
wild? There are many books on reflexology and it will be worth
your while to pick one up.

Here's how the magic works:

It begins after your lover takes a shower (preferably with you)
and you begin your erotic massage from the feet up. Just as you
would work on his hands (see Gemini), now you knead, pull
and stroke your lover's feet. Just follow the chart on reflexology.
For instance, the big toe connects to the head and the center of
the foot, when massaged this will effect the stomach, kidneys
and pancreas. Yes, really!

Give special attention to that sensitive spot at the back of his
ankle right above the heel. The area around the heel leads to the
sexual organs. If he moans blissfully while you're caressing this
area, you'll be doing it right. And let your thumbs knead the
sole of his feet, adding at least five years to his life.

Most important, never massage one foot and not the other.

Everything in life and love is balance!

How will your lover react to a foot massage? Well, not many men are treated to this delicious sensual experience and by the time you work your way up his leg and reach his inner thigh, he should be having a deep conversation with God.

Don't forget to dim the lights at the outset and put some magical sounds on the stereo. Actually, for this particular water sign, a tape of ocean waves, with gulls in the background, will be just perfect.

WHERE IS THAT ROMANTIC GETAWAY?

There are mini cruises which last a weekend or incredible vessels that take you to the Mediterranean in total luxury. Now Olivia knows which one you prefer, but whichever one you can afford will be delightful for your Pisces.

Here Pisces is in his element, surrounded by shimmering water, puffy white clouds in blue skies and tanned, loving you. That's about all he needs to believe he's won the lottery.

After dinner you stroll on the deck, hand in hand. Very little is said between you, because you are both so in tune with each other's feelings. Later, in your cabin, you will lie in your lover's arms, gently swayed by the rhymthic ocean, and you will have the sensation that you're a million miles away from reality. That's exactly where you are...in a fantasy world where emotions are intensified, where every caress is felt to its core.

Then your bodies begin to move to the same rhythmic motion...slowly, always slowly...and when you open your eyes, the moonlight streaming in through the porthole, will be on your lover's face...and as he smiles down at you...lovingly, adoringly...you close your eyes again...knowing the image of that smile will stay in your heart always...

HOW TO PLEASE PISCES SEXUALLY.

Your Pisces lover has a side of him that you might not have discovered as yet. It's wonderfully submissive and erotic. He wants to be controlled.

What Olivia has in mind will give him the ultimate feeling of adventure because he won't know what's coming next. He will also feel guilt-free indulging in the most outrageous sexual acts because he's just following your instructions. It's like a little boy getting permission from his mother to play in the mud and get wonderfully, deliciously dirty.

Naturally, you don't have to explain any of this psycho-sexual strategy to him. Let this be just between us. All he'll know is that you're awakening primal instincts in him that he has long suppressed. Instincts he wouldn't dare articulate to anyone. The lovely thing about erotic sex is that it doesn't have to be spoken, only felt.

So the first thing you must do begins before your next date. Tell your Pisces that you are planning to orchestrate the evening. What's the plan, he asks? It will all be in the instructions, you say.

What instructions?

They will come in the mail, you answer.

Say not another word.

The following is the first instruction you will mail your lover before your date, explaining that he is *to do your bidding* exactly as told.

Instruction #1

This is where you tell him to go into his apartment and take off all his clothes. Describe in detail how he is to remove them and, at the point when he takes off his undershorts, he is thinking about you...to let his hand caress his own hardness and to give in to the anticipation of what lies ahead, as he telephones you and listens to your taped message.

Give him the exact time to do this, down to the second. If he misses the precise moment, the evening is called off.

The message should tell him where to find the next message. "It's in the brown shoes in your bedroom closet," etc.

Instruction #2

Instruct him to head for the nearest thing to a low-down, honkey-tonk bar on the edge of town. Tell him the exact time to be there. Again, if he is even one minute off, the night is over.

Now if you're too cautious for this colorful scenario, it can easily be changed to one of the most elegant hotel bars. The choice is yours. If the latter appeals to you, you might consider a room for the night to go along with the final instructions.

When he arrives at this magic moment, he will find you sit-

ting at the bar. Tell him to have a drink, and hand him a note.
Immediately leave.

Instruction #3

The note tells him to finish his drink and the exact time at
which to call you. Remind him that timing is everything. When
he calls, tell him how you took off your clothes, piece by piece
as you entered your apartment. Explain how excited you are
knowing that he's coming over. Tell him that you're about to
take a bath and you expect him to be there, to dry you off.
"Be there, on time...hurry."

Tell him you'll leave the door open and that you're giving
him exactly so many minutes to get there. Or the door locks. If
there's a traffic jam or a helicopter lands on the highway, he
loses for the night. You'll just have to start the game over again
on another night. If this does happen, refuse to discuss the game
until the next date and the next message.
If all goes well and he arrives on time, have him lock the door
behind him.
You can play the game as long as you want. At this point it's
optional. What Olivia can guarantee is that if he's followed the
rules perfectly until now...if his timing has been flawless...if
he's as hot as you are...it's *your* turn to perform.
If you need any inspiration in this area, just read the other
eleven signs.

Share the fantasy...

Another of your lover's secrets is his desire to watch.
So with your bathtub overflowing with bubbles, the bathroom
steamy and a small red light in the fixture, have him sit down
without touching you.
Now gently draw your knees up and reach your hand into the
warm below the bubbles. Let him watch your face as you fantasize whatever pictures you need in order to climax. Hopefully,
given the erotic situation that you find yourself in, that will be
all it takes to bring pleasure to yourself -- and to your lover,
while he satisfies himself while watching you.

ASTROLOGY ORDER FORM

**Know your lover's true erotic nature. Fill out the enclosed
form and send it, along with $20.00, in check or money order to:**

Olivia
c/o Victoria House Press
67 Wall Street Ste. 2411
New York, New York 10005

You will receive a computerized in-depth astrological portrait,
approximately 20 pages, based on your lover's sun sign.

_____

Name

_____

Date of birth   Hour   Minute

_____

City and State of birth

_____

Country

Send Astrological Portrait to:

_____

Name

_____

Street

_____

City   State   Zip

ASTROLOGY ORDER FORM

Know your lover's true erotic nature. Fill out the enclosed form and send it, along with $20.00, in check or money order to:

Olivia
c/o Victoria House Press
67 Wall Street Ste. 2411
New York, New York 10005

You will receive a computerized in-depth astrological portrait, approximately 20 pages, based on your lover's sun sign.

_____

Name

_____

Date of birth   Hour   Minute

_____

City and State of birth

_____

Country

Send Astrological Portrait to:

_____

Name

_____

Street

_____

City   State   Zip

ASTROLOGY ORDER FORM

**Know your lover's true erotic nature. Fill out the enclosed
form and send it, along with $20.00, in check or money order to:**

Olivia
c/o Victoria House Press
67 Wall Street Ste. 2411
New York, New York 10005

You will receive a computerized in-depth astrological portrait,
approximately 20 pages, based on your lover's sun sign.

Name

Date of birth   Hour   Minute

City and State of birth

Country

Send Astrological Portrait to:

Name

Street

City   State   Zip

ASTROLOGY ORDER FORM

**Know your lover's true erotic nature. Fill out the enclosed
form and send it, along with $20.00, in check or money order to:**

Olivia
c/o Victoria House Press
67 Wall Street Ste. 2411
New York, New York 10005

You will receive a computerized in-depth astrological portrait,
approximately 20 pages, based on your lover's sun sign.

_____

Name

_____

Date of birth   Hour   Minute

_____

City and State of birth

_____

Country

Send Astrological Portrait to:

_____

Name

_____

Street

_____

City   State   Zip

Erotic Astrology

ASTROLOGY ORDER FORM

Know your lover's true erotic nature. Fill out the enclosed form and send it, along with $20.00, in check or money order to:

Olivia
c/o Victoria House Press
67 Wall Street Ste. 2411
New York, New York 10005

You will receive a computerized in-depth astrological portrait, approximately 20 pages, based on your lover's sun sign.

_____
Name

_____
Date of birth   Hour   Minute

_____
City and State of birth

_____
Country

Send Astrological Portrait to:

_____
Name

_____
Street

_____
City   State   Zip

ASTROLOGY ORDER FORM

Know your lover's true erotic nature. Fill out the enclosed form and send it, along with $20.00, in check or money order to:

Olivia
c/o Victoria House Press
67 Wall Street Ste. 2411
New York, New York 10005

You will receive a computerized in-depth astrological portrait, approximately 20 pages, based on your lover's sun sign.

_____

Name

_____

Date of birth   Hour   Minute

_____

City and State of birth

_____

Country

Send Astrological Portrait to:

_____

Name

_____

Street

_____

City   State   Zip